Adam and His Kin
The Lost History of Their Lives and Times

Ruth Beechick

MOTT MEDIA
Fenton, Michigan

Cover art by: Robert Fobear

Text illustrations by: Michael Denman

© by Ruth Beechick

All rights in this book are reserved. No portion of this book may be reproduced in any form, electronic or mechanical, including photocopy, recording or any information storage and retrieval system, without permission in writing from the publisher, except for small portions as needed in reviewing or critiquing the book. For information write Mott Media, 1130 Fenway Circle, Fenton, Michigan 48430.

For information about other Mott Media publications visit our website at www.mottmedia.com

Printed by Color House Graphics, Grand Rapids, Michigan, USA.

ISBN-13: 978-0-940319-07-3
ISBN-10: 0-940319-07-1

Contents

Preface 1
1. The Beginning of Time 5
2. In the Garden 11
3. The Punishment 17
4. Adam's Children 23
5. Cain 30
6. Writing in the Stars 37
7. The Preachers 45
8. Noah 53
9. The Year of 1656 59
10. The Great Flood 64
11. The Calendar Puzzle 70
12. Starting Up the New World 76
13. Trouble at Ararat 82
14. Land of the Two Rivers 88
15. The Tower of Bel 96
16. Aftermath 103
17. Gods and Goddesses 109
18. The Death of Noah 116
19. Abram 126

Appendices
A. Writers of Genesis 137
B. Genesis 1:1 to 11:27a 139
C. Study Projects 153
D. Annotated Bibliography 157

Preface

The purpose of this book is to provide a simple narrative of the events of the period of time covered in the opening chapters of Genesis. Information from various sources is merged with that of the Bible itself. And to add color, a little imagination is used in describing what a person might have said or done in a situation.

This format conveys some ideas that are easily missed when reading the brief facts given in Genesis—for instance, the idea of the overlapping of generations in those times or the idea of a completely lost world which has not even left a trace of the original Tigris and Euphrates Rivers. This style is similar to a preacher's illustration whereby he expands on a basic idea from Scripture.

A limitation of narrating is that the writer, unlike a commentator, cannot provide two or more options for interpreting a passage. She must choose one and proceed with the story. Therefore I ask my readers' understanding on problems where there are honest differences of opinion—questions such as who were the sons of God who married the daughters of men. You are certainly free to disagree with me and tell the story differently at some points.

Having spent thirteen years writing Sunday school lessons and hearing from concerned teachers that we were adding to the Scripture if the donkey went "clop, clop," it was difficult for me to begin this work. At first I wrote that "maybe" Adam and Eve walked in the garden on their first day, "perhaps" they enjoyed the flowers, and so forth. Later I realized that I couldn't annoy my readers with "maybe" all through the story. So I have decided to say one big "maybe" here in the preface and hope that will suffice.

Secular history books do not balk at guessing. It is common for a writer to say that several centuries must have passed because one artifact he examined is stone, while another is copper. Or an archeologist may say that several millennia of development must have preceded his findings because he uncovered some writing or sculpture, and people could not learn to write or sculpt like that in a short time. Events are moved around as needed to fit the preconceived evolutionary idea of history—that man began as a brute and slowly raised himself to a higher kind of life. So if we begin with the preconceived idea that man began as a God-like creature, made in the very image of God, we, too, should set events in what we believe is their most likely position.

It is not unreasonable to postulate a short history for man such as this book does. Recently Egyptologist David Rohl, in his book *Pharaohs and Kings*, proposed shortening the traditional Egyptian chronology by several hundred years, echoing an earlier such proposal by Immanuel Velikovsky. Also historian and archeologist Peter James (*Centuries of Darkness*) proposes shortening the chronology of several other Mediterranean civilizations to better fit the actual data of a century of archeology, rather than tying these chronologies to an obviously flawed Egyptian chronology, as is the current practice.

Another fascinating book along this line is *After the Flood* by historian Bill Cooper, which is a study of pre-Christian European historical records. The ancient pagans did not have the book of Genesis to draw on, yet five nations studied here traced their genealogy back to Noah. Several ancient chronologers, some working from classical literature and some from astronomy, and as far apart as the Irish and the Mayas, all point to the beginning of the world at about 4000 to 5000 B.C.

Thus the Bible's time frame is corroborated by numerous independent historical records. In this short time frame, we can look at the beginning of civilizations and see mankind simply rebuilding society after the Great Flood or after the catastrophic

Preface 3

judgment at Babel, which two events were only about a century apart. This rebuilding by intelligent humans who already had knowledge and skills would take only a generation or two. It would not require a long, slow process of evolving from grunting cave men to civilized people who could speak and farm and build, as history books so commonly imply.

The big problems of early history are not solved in this book. I have simply tried to place events where they seem to fit best. The changing of the year from 360 days to a longer year is another of those problems. I have placed that as one event in the Flood year, even though Velikovsky (in *Worlds in Collision*) places it in the eighth or seventh century B.C. and Cooper suggests there may be several catastrophic, calendar-changing events. Most other historians—and astronomers— take the uniformitarian view that the year has always been as it now is.

Performing some simple arithmetic on the birth dates in the Genesis genealogy brings one to the date of 1656 for the Great Flood. But that procedure assumes that each son was born exactly on his father's birthday, and since they probably weren't, we could use an adjusted date of 1660. But did the ancient record keepers look at ages in the same way we do? Did they, perhaps, mean something like "In the year that Adam became 130, he begat Seth"? If so, 1656 remains the biblical date for the Flood.

The most arbitrary liberty I took with historical events was placing the appearance of the supernova Vela X at the disaster of Babel. Some ancient writings and drawings indicate the Sumerians knew of this spectacular event, but little else seems to have been written about it in ancient times. Thus we have no clear historical record of the supernova which modern astronomers have since rediscovered. Uniformitarian astronomy would date this supernova at a time before the heavens were even created according to our "young earth" time frame. Thus I chose to place it at the Babel event. Since society and writing itself were then in upheaval, it would be understandable that no one left a clear account of it.

If I waited until all the problems were solved, the book would never be finished. So I offer it as it is, hoping that it helps some readers to a better understanding of the Bible.

I owe much to writers who have preceded me, particularly those listed in the bibliography, and most particularly Dr. Henry Morris, whose books have greatly influenced my thinking over the years. I wish to thank my good friend Dr. D. Chris Benner, a physics professor at William and Mary College and a NASA researcher. Although he doesn't agree with everything in this book, he helped me with problems in astronomy, and through his thoughtful comments on the manuscript he saved it from some mistakes it otherwise would have had. I thank my friend Audre D. Fox for translating a German article. And I thank several in my own family, who always are my best critics and supporters. Sons Allen and Andy solved computer problems to make the job easier, and along with daughters-in-law, Ellen and Janice, were wonderful help by commenting on the manuscript, by discussing problems and possibilities and by believing in the usefulness of such a book as this.

Readers who want people in their story immediately may flip over the first few pages for now, and come back to them later. Adam and his wife begin their honeymoon by chapter 2.

Ruth Beechick

1. The Beginning of Time

Once there was no time. A misty curtain hides that from our view and no living person can send his thoughts there and back, unless it be a little child.

Then God created the heavens and the earth. Out of nothing He created them, and in that instant time began, time for all the space of the heavens and for all the matter of earth. Only God knew that first instant of time.

On one side of the curtain, the eternity side, space and matter were not and could not be, but on the other side, now came time and space and matter in the creative act of God. Matter filled the darkness of space like a watery vapor and God's Spirit moved back and forth upon it.

God said, "Light be," and there was light, coming as on wings of His words, spreading into space and shining in time.

God looked at the light and saw that it was good. He separated it from darkness, and as God's light dawned in the first morning of time, God announced that light was called Day and darkness was called Night. Thus passed a full day, with its evening and morning, and the calendar of time began to count the days.

So says the history book of earth. He who someday reads the history book of angels may read that next God created angels to dwell in His glorious light. Angels first opened their eyes and beheld the pure light of God and the newly-made waters.

In earth's history it was now the second day and God said, "Sky be; divide the waters." Bright angels of God watched in awe

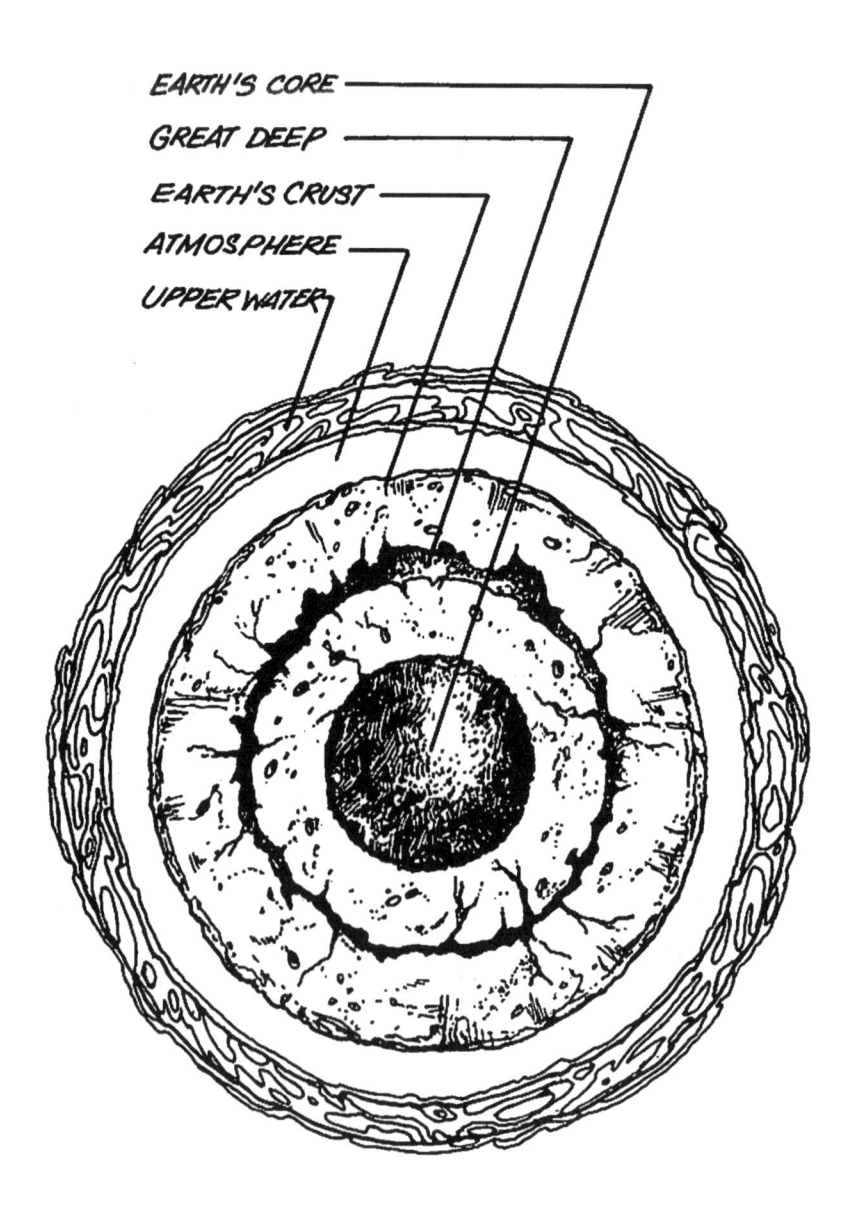

- EARTH'S CORE
- GREAT DEEP
- EARTH'S CRUST
- ATMOSPHERE
- UPPER WATER

as a sky stretched out, dividing the waters. God measured the sky with the span of His hand. Above the sky hung the upperwater and below the sky, measured in the hollow of God's hand, was the great deep, formed within the circle of His compass. It was a beautiful ocean of liquid water. The sky between the upper water and the lower water God called Heaven.

Evening passed and morning came, and time counted its second day.

On the third day, angels moved into places where they could see, as people do before a parade, ready for rejoicing and singing and celebrating. It was the glorious day for laying the foundations of the earth.

God said, "Let the waters under the sky be gathered together into one place and let dry land appear." Upon wings of His words earth's cornerstone was laid, the foundation fastened, and the dust of dry land reached out above the waters. Hills and fields were measured in their places, mountains settled, and water flowed into the boundaries God set for them. In the fountains of the deep, God shut the doors, and on the circle of the earth He told the waves to go so far and no farther.

All the angels shouted for joy. God called the dry land Earth and He called the gathered waters Seas, and God saw that they were good.

Next, God said, "Let the earth bring forth grass, and bushes with their seeds, and trees with fruit, each with its own kind of seed." And the earth did, and God saw that this too was good.

Evening passed, morning came, and another day was ended.

On the fourth day, God said, "Let there be lights in the sky to divide the day from the night." He made a great light to rule over Day, beaming God's light upon the earth, and He made a lesser light for Night.

God made stars also, the constellations in their places, and the wandering stars—the planets—to move in their own paths.

The vast heavens He filled with stars of light. He knew how many there were, and He knew them all by name. They made a road for the sun and mansions for the moon. They ruled Night and began telling the glory of God and the work of His hands. The morning stars sang together while the angels shouted for joy.

"Let the lights be for signs," God said, "and for seasons, and for days, and years." God saw that they were good. The lights ruled while evening and morning passed, and the fourth day of time was ended.

On earth gentle waves splashed on the beaches, soft winds blew across tender grasses, plants opened their flowers to the light of a new dawn, but no voice was heard on land or sea. In all earth's beauty there was nothing with life and mind of its own to decide to pick a flower or to nibble on a blade of grass, no creature to taste cool water or to sing God's praises. Angels hushed to watch the day in awe.

God said, "Let the waters bring forth moving, living creatures, and let birds fly above the earth in the open sky." He created giant sea monsters with life, and middle-sized sea creatures with life, and small creatures with life, each like its own kind, all swarming abundantly in the seas and knowing they were alive. And He created living birds. Small wings fluttered and broad wings glided through the sky that was only three days old. Chirping and chattering and singing mixed with crowing, clucking, and honking, as all kinds of birds tried out their syringes. They, too, knew they were alive.

God saw that this was good. He blessed all the fish and birds and said, "Be fruitful and multiply. Fill the seas and the earth." Evening passed and morning came and the fifth day of time was finished.

Earth was rotating once each day. Moon and sun were traveling along the paths so carefully marked for them in the starry heavens. Nothing was out of place, and it was the sixth day of time.

God said, "Let the earth bring forth living creatures after their kinds," and earth could do that. Matter had been created and life had been created, and now God made domestic animals, wild animals, and kinds to creep upon the earth. Large gray animals began to walk slowly about. Graceful smaller animals began to run. Animals played and brayed and chattered and barked. Every animal knew that it was alive. God saw that they were very good.

Then God, the three-in-one, said to Himself, "Let us make mankind in our image, after our likeness. And let them rule over the fish of the sea, the birds of the air, the tame beasts and all the earth, and every creeping thing on the earth."

God used dust of the ground to form a body for the man. Animal life was not high enough for man, so God breathed into his nostrils the spirit of life that made him in the image of God. Man became a living soul. The spirit breathed into him by God was glorious to behold. It shone through the body of the man, clothing him in shining light. The man had a mind that thought some of the same thoughts as God, that understood what God said, and that could form his own thoughts into speech.

God put the man in a garden He planted in Eden. A wonderful garden it was. A paradise! Green-boughed trees stood straight and tall among spreading broad-leaved trees, some with flowers and some with fruits good for eating. All were pleasant. In the middle of the garden was the Tree of Life and the Tree of Knowing Good and Evil. God told the man to care for the garden and to eat of its fruits, all that he wanted, except for one, the Tree of Knowing Good and Evil. Don't eat of that tree, God said, for in the day the man eats of it he would surely die.

God brought to the man beasts that had come from the ground, and birds, too, to see what the man would call them. The man had a name—Man, or Adam. Now he was to name the other creatures.

Along came a bushy-tailed animal with a long, pointed nose and perky ears. Adam named it fox. A big, colorless animal he named elephant.

Down flew a bird the color of the midday sky, and Adam had

to think a moment. He hadn't named any colors yet, but this was a good time to start. "Bluebird," he said. Adam continued, naming the osprey, the eagle, the raccoon, and the huge, lumbering behemoth with a tail like a cedar tree. Whatever the man called each creature, that was its name. The vocabulary of the Edenese language grew larger every minute.

Adam named domestic animals, beasts made for the field, and birds of the sky. They all were friendly with the man and he was friendly with them. Each animal had a mate of its own kind, but there was no mate for Adam. Evening was nearing, and no creature was yet found that could think and talk like Adam or be a helper and partner for him. He was alone.

God already knew that. Now that the man knew it too, God said, "It is not good that the man should be alone; I will make a helpmate for him." God caused a deep sleep to fall upon the man.

Then He took a piece of Adam's side and closed up the space again. From the piece, God formed the helper.

When the man awoke, there was a beautiful wife fresh from the hand of God. He was rather good at naming now, and he said, "She is made from my flesh and bones. She shall be called woman, because she was taken out of man."

God blessed the man and woman. He said, "Have children and fill the earth. Learn all about the earth, and rule over the fish and birds and animals. Look, I have given you all the plants and trees to be food for you, and I have given grasses and plants to be food for the birds and animals."

God saw everything He had made, and it was very good. It was finished. Evening and morning of the sixth day passed. Nightfall announced the start of the seventh day. On that day God rested, and He blessed the seventh day and made it holy because that was when He ceased from all His work which He created and made.

The man and his wife began their honeymoon in the beautiful garden in the land of Eden.

2. In the Garden

Walking in the shade of trees along the river, Adam and his wife tasted delicious fruits and talked long and intensely about God who created them the day before. They approached the middle of the garden, and Adam warned his wife about a certain tree there.

"It's called the Tree of Knowing Good and Evil," he told her. "The Lord God said that we may freely eat of all the trees in the garden except that one, for in the day that we eat of it we shall surely die."

Neither the man nor the woman wanted to eat of that tree. If God said No, then No it would be. Their hearts were full of love for their Creator who had put them in this pure and happy and perfect place.

The sun sank low in the sky and the rosy glow of day began turning into the deep magenta of night. Coolness settled over the garden and God came to talk with the man and his wife. They felt His love wrap around them and rejoiced in the thought that every seventh day was to be holy like this.

The days that followed were work days. Each morning Adam and his wife awoke to music of the morning stars while the rose-gold sun gently bathed their garden in its light. It was pure pleasure for them to learn to care for their wonderful garden and to rule over it.

They called green-branched trees cedars and firs and pines. Another kind was named sycamores. Each kind of fruit tree and flowering tree also received a name of its own, and all the smaller plants, too. With names, it was easier to think about the trees and plants and to talk about them. Words like smooth, green and leafy helped too, as well as words like bark and stems and fronds. When the people ate fruit, they made words like sweet and sour, and like delicious and favorite.

Adam was very intelligent. He could easily see wonderful pattern and design in God's creation. He studied the smallest parts of plants and understood that God holds them together, and he saw how each plant fit into the larger scheme of the garden and its inhabitants of animals and people. Everything Adam learned about the garden taught him more about the garden's Creator.

Some plants were for eating and some seemed, instead, to be for the spirit. Flowers were the latter kind. They wore especially beautiful raiment, and perfume as well. Lovely as the flowers were, Adam and his wife were more lovely yet, dressed as they were with the radiant light of the spirit. Yet the two gardeners were delighted with the flowers.

On one budding vine the flowers remained closed. "When will they open?" asked the woman after observing the vine for several days.

"Wait until the full moon," said Adam.

The moon grew larger and larger, and on the night when it was about to rise in the acme of its full round form, Adam and his wife sat before the vine silently, sensing that a spoken word might cause them to miss what they had come to see. Surrounded by the music of delightful nighttime, they waited. Then just as the glowing moon emerged from below the horizon, flowers on the vine began to stir. Outer petals gracefully spread themselves, and inner petals followed, layer after layer, until at last the luxuriant flowers were fully opened and basking in the light of the moon that was as round as they.

"Moonflower," said the woman. She could name things too.

All was harmony in the garden. Animals and people liked each

In the Garden 13

other. The two people learned to swim like the beaver, to climb trees like the bear, to hop like the rabbit, and to run like the deer. They rode elephants and horses. As time went on they watched little chicks hatch and cuddled tiny kittens. Play and work mingled together, with no way to tell which was which.

When God visited in the evenings, Adam had opportunity to ask why God had made him and to learn that it was so he could love and enjoy God forever. He asked how the earth and heavens came to be and listened raptly while God told him about the first days of creation.

He asked about God Himself. How did God come to be? What was it like outside of time where God lived? And those answers he could not understand. "I am that I am." God was eternal, uncreated. Adam learned more each day, but, intelligent as he was, his mind was not big enough to fully comprehend God.

It was easier to understand the plan of the universe. Adam could intuitively see that the sun, moon and stars followed certain paths, and he could keep track of the days and months that passed. He began learning important signs in the stars, and he saw the glory of God written in all the heavenly bodies.

While the two citizens of Eden were managing their earthly responsibilities, angels worked at their heavenly tasks. The most powerful angel in heaven was Lucifer. So beautiful was he that he was called son of the morning. And so beautiful and powerful was he that pride exalted his opinion of himself. He began to think that God had not created him. On the day he first opened his eyes, water was everywhere. It pleased him more to think that he evolved from the water than to think that God created him. He, then, must be a god too.

After contemplating this, he decided that he would become the highest power. He would exalt himself above the stars of God. In the sides of the north, above the heights of the clouds, he would be like the most High. He talked to other angels about his plan. God had not created them, Lucifer said, so they didn't have to obey

God. They were gods themselves. One-third of the angels decided to join Lucifer in his rebellion.

War broke out in heaven, and God's faithful angels fought the rebels. In the end Lucifer and his army lost their first battle. No longer leader of the worshipers of God in Heaven, Lucifer was now the proud leader of the rebellious angels.

He plotted to fight his war on the earth, to get people to join his rebellion. To do so he would violate the natural realms where God had put His creatures. Although Lucifer was made for the heavenly realm and man was made for the earthly realm, he decided to cross the boundary between. And he would do it immediately, before people spread all over the earth.

Thus it happened that one day in the garden, when the man and wife were near the Tree of Knowing Good and Evil, there came a serpent, a charming and intelligent creature with scales glistening in the sun and wings lifting him to an upright position. He spoke softly to the woman. "Did God say you shall not eat of every tree in the garden?"

The woman, not startled in the least at the serpent's approach, thought about his question. Why did God deny them that fruit? The first sliver of discontent that she had ever known slipped into her mind. She answered, "We may eat fruit from all the trees except this one in the middle of the garden, we shall not eat of it, nor shall we touch it, lest we die."

Lucifer gloated within himself. How smart he had been not to say, "Woman, please help me rebel against God." She would certainly not have agreed to that. But his chosen strategy of leading her little by little was already working. Hadn't she made God's commandment harsher by adding the part about not touching the fruit? And hadn't she made the penalty weaker by not saying that they will surely die? She only said "lest we die." He would try another step.

"You won't die," the serpent said. "God knows that when

In the Garden 15

you eat the fruit your eyes will be opened and you will be as gods, knowing good and evil."

The woman contemplated the tree. Its fruit looked pleasant and good to eat. Would it really make her wise like God, knowing good and evil? She stepped in for a closer look. Then she picked a fruit. Turning it around in her hand, it seemed a small matter if she should taste it. Just one little bite. And so she did.

At that moment, the spirit within her died. Its radiance faded, and she stood beside the tree feeling helpless and naked. The serpent quickly disappeared. He was not going to help her. "That deceiver!" she exclaimed. She did know evil. That much of the serpent's words came true. And how terrible it was! Evil was inside her. Could she throw away the fruit? Could she cough up the bite and spit it out? Could she undo her act in any way?

No, it was done. She couldn't restore her innocence.

Adam must eat the fruit too. He must not leave her alone in this condition. Frightened and distraught, she ran to Adam, the remains of the fruit still in her hand. Seeing her pitiful state, Adam needed no explanation. Her confused words, her crying, her begging tore at his heart.

Adam well understood that eating the fruit meant death. How would God handle it if He had one human with life and one who had lost life? Would Adam be alone again without a mate? He did not wait to ask God what should be done, but decided to share in the woman's fate. He took the fruit from her hand and ate it.

Now Adam, too, lost his glory and stood naked and afraid. Edenese as yet had no words to describe the shame and guilt they were now feeling. They pulled large leaves off a fig tree and sewed them together as best they could to make garments for themselves. That outer covering helped their feelings a little, but did nothing for the guilt and fear inside.

How easily they had fallen for the wiles of Lucifer! Adam and his wife now understood that he had led them into death and not into better knowledge, as he promised. He was a liar. He was not a friend but an enemy.

So disturbed were their minds that they could not proceed with their chores or any useful activity. They walked agitatedly or huddled in bushes, dreading the coming of God, who surely would have to kill them now.

3. The Punishment

In the cool of that evening, Adam and his wife heard the voice of God as He was walking in the garden. They quickly hid among the trees.

God called out, "Adam, where are you?" Adam answered, "I heard Your voice in the garden, and I was afraid, because I was naked, so I hid myself." God said, "Who told you that you were naked? Have you eaten of the tree that I told you not to eat from?"

Adam, shaking with fear and with resentment toward his wife, could not simply admit, "I ate it." Instead, he said, "The woman whom you put here with me—she gave me fruit of the tree, and I ate it."

Then God spoke to the woman. "What is this that you have done?" The woman, like Adam, could not take the blame herself. She said, "The serpent deceived me, and I ate it." Then God sorrowfully, spoke words He had to speak. To the serpent He said, "Because you have done this, you are cursed more than all animals. You will go on your belly and eat off the dust all the days of your life." Thus the clever and beautiful serpent, the one who among all animals could most charm the woman, was to become a slithering snake and frightful dragon.

Next, God spoke to the enemy angel who was in the serpent.

> I will put enmity between you and the woman
> And between your seed and her Seed.

> Her child will crush your head
> And you will crush his heel.

The angel heard in those words that he and people were going to be enemies. The woman and her descendants were not going to be on his side, God had said. Well, he would prove God wrong. He would win the woman's children just as easily as he had won the woman herself.

What else had God said? That a child of the woman's was going to crush his head, and he would only crush the heel of the child? Well, he would change that part, too. He would hunt this child and hound him to the death. He would see to it that no child of the woman ever crushed his head. This was war, and he determined to win.

The man and woman still stood before God feeling guilty and ashamed. They did, indeed, have knowledge of evil now. Whereas before they ate the forbidden fruit they knew only good, now they knew both good and evil, and it didn't make them feel like gods. If only they could make the choice over again!

The woman already hated the serpent. Why had he deceived her so? Could she ever get rid of the evil he had brought?

What had God said? Was the woman to have a child? Then she was not going to die now. Maybe there was hope. Adam and his wife listened intently to the words.

God continued, and now he was talking to the woman. "You will have more sorrow in bearing children, and your desire will be to your husband and he will rule over you."

Yes, thought the woman, she should have let Adam decide about the fruit. She should have listened to her husband and to God, instead of to the serpent.

Next, God spoke to Adam. "Because you listened to your wife and ate of the tree of which I commanded you not to eat, cursed is the ground for you. In sorrow shall you eat of it all the days of your life. Thorns and thistles shall it bring forth. By the sweat of your

The Punishment

brow shall you eat bread until you return to the ground from which you were taken. For dust you are, and to dust shall you return."

In deep sorrow Adam pondered the curses. Through a long silence he stood, numbed by the enormity of it all. Death had come to the kingdom which had been all light and happiness just a short time before. Were his eyes failing or was the light of the sun actually fading, as it seemed? The encroaching darkness around Adam matched the darkness within him.

After a while he began to reflect upon the hope in God's words. The Seed of the woman, what would he do? Somehow that child would crush the evil serpent, and not only the garden's serpent but the power behind the serpent, that evil angel who had held a high place in the spiritual realm. That much Adam realized. Would he then be freed from the evil within him? Would the earth be freed from its curses?

Adam didn't understand exactly what God meant, but he thought about the promise and believed it. The promise was like a glimmer of light in his dark mind. Something was reborn within him.

Now he could think toward the future. His wife was going to bear children, and through her the promised Seed would come. There swept over Adam a wave of tenderness toward the woman, replacing his earlier anger and resentment. She would be the mother of the living, the mother of all who would hold onto God's promise, as he now was. Through her would come the Seed, and the hope of deliverance from the terrible death that he had tasted today.

He must name the woman Life, or Eve. Speaking aloud, he said to her, "You are Eve, the mother of all living."

The Lord God returned to the pair. They watched soberly as God set up stones for an altar and selected two male sheep and killed them. They were dismayed to see blood spurt from these animal friends as they fell lifeless. They had never seen death like this before. Physical death. The sight cut deeply into Adam's heart and mind as he began to comprehend the tragedy of his disobedience. It should be Eve and him being killed just now. But God killed these sheep instead.

What a mercy God was showing to him! Love for God mingled with the horror of death, and Adam was so full of emotion he could not speak. The garden was now defiled with death and he was helpless to change it. He saw how blood was sprinkled on all sides of the altar, the animals were skinned, and pieces of the carcasses were arranged upon wood on the altar. When everything was ready, fire came and burned the offering. The aroma rose up toward heaven.

From the skins, God made garments for Adam and Eve and clothed them. These clothes would not last forever. They would wear out and more animals would be killed. Blood and death, again and again. Maybe the substitution of the sheep's blood for his own blood would not last forever either. Is this what the future held? The sacrifice of an animal for himself, again and again? Adam's mind slowly began to digest what God was teaching him. He dimly understood that the promised Seed would someday be the answer to all this. That Seed would bring an end to death.

The day had begun like all others in Adam's short life—with warm peace and love and joy, with happy work, and with the anticipation of a walk with God in the evening. He woke up clothed in glory and knowing only good. Now he stood in his animal-skin garment, his body headed toward death, and his mind and heart contaminated with the knowledge of evil.

With regret, Adam considered the changes. But there was yet more. God now asked him and Eve to leave the garden.

They begged, "Please, Lord God, let us stay." They didn't think just then of the Tree of Life in the garden and how terrible it would be if they ate its fruit and lived forever in their fallen condition. They implored God to let them stay in the garden.

So it was necessary for God to drive Adam and Eve out of the garden.

The Punishment

At the eastern entrance of the garden, God placed two cherubim. These awesome heavenly creatures stood upright like men. Their hands were like those of a man, but the soles of their feet were like the soles of a calf, and they sparkled like polished brass.

Each cherub had four faces and looked in all directions. On one side was the face of a man, a man like Adam, but with heavenly glory added. On the right of that was the face of a lion, like one of the splendid beasts of the field. On the left side was the face of an ox like the strong work animal which God had made for man. And on the fourth side was the face of an eagle like the most majestic of birds that fly in the air. With four faces, the cherubim could go in any direction straight ahead without turning, and they could move like flashes of fire.

Each of the living creatures had four wings. With two they covered their bodies, and two they spread out on high. The wings of one could touch the spread wings of the other. These cherubim were brilliant like burning coals. Bright fire moved back and forth between them, and from the fire a flaming sword flashed and guarded the entrance to the garden.

Adam and Eve, almost blinded by the shining display of God's glory, fell on their faces and could not speak. For them the cherubim represented both the presence of God and His separation from them. Now this gate was as close as they could get to God. The sword was a flaming reminder that they could not enter anymore.

At last, exhausted, Adam and Eve walked slowly away. The air felt chillier, the night darker than any they had yet known.

Within a few days they chose a location in which to settle, and began to plant a garden. With heavy hearts they tried to make their garden as good as God's, but they never succeeded.

They followed the pattern of working for six days and keeping the seventh day holy. On holy days Adam went to the garden gate, and there, before the cherubim, he offered sacrifices as God had taught him.

So numbed with grief were Adam and Eve, that they could scarcely think about the curses which had brought such changes in their lives. But those other words of God in the garden, those words about the promised Seed, were turned over in their minds continually. They wanted to understand everything they could about the words.

That Seed seemed the only thing worth living for now. They must wait and watch for the child God would send. Only that child could turn back evil and death from the world.

How soon would he come?

4. Adam's Children

Weeks of work and Sabbaths of rest began to ease the pain in the hearts of Adam and Eve. Their life outside the garden began to seem almost normal, and the memory of Paradise grew dim.

One day they realized that Eve was going to have a child, and they were happier than they had been since that most terrible day. God's promise was coming true now, it seemed. Very soon the Seed would arrive.

In due time the baby was born and it was a little boy. Eve said, "I have gotten a manchild from the Lord." And when she said the word *gotten* it sounded, in their Edenese language, like Cain. That's what she would name the boy—Cain.

The boy grew only a little before the parents noticed that he could disobey and do wrong. At times he stubbornly wanted his own way. *Just like us*, thought both Adam and Eve. They were disappointed. He was not going to be the promised Seed.

Later another baby boy was born and Eve named him *Vapor*, or *Vanity*. It was pronounced *Abel*. She now understood more about the world and its curse. Everything was vanity. Life was like a vapor, like the morning mist, which hung in the air for awhile and then vanished. Death would come to Cain, to Adam and her, and to this newest baby. They all would vanish.

More children were born to Adam and Eve, both boys and girls, and the parents diligently taught them about God. One day Adam came home from offering a sacrifice, and he had in his hands the story of God creating the heavens and the earth. It was God's own words, he said. Now he could be sure to teach it to his children exactly right. And they could teach their children exactly right. People couldn't forget or mix it up.

Other times Adam came home with exciting new insights into the promise. The Seed would be a God-man, he told Eve, not a baby of theirs who could do wrong just like them. Prophecies were written in the sky, and Adam was learning how to read them. He could read there that the Seed would be born of a virgin. A Star would arise with ruling power in his hand—the Sun of righteousness with healing in his wings.

Adam made his children memorize God's prophecy given in the garden. "This tells the history of the world until the end of its days," Adam told them. "Learn it well, and teach it to your children too."

> I will put enmity between you and the woman
> And between your seed and her Seed.

To explain that part, Adam had to teach his children that God was speaking to the rebellious angel. People who follow his ways will be his seed, and they will always war against the promised Seed. Throughout the history of the world, this rebel, this enemy of man will try to conquer the Seed, but he will succeed only in bruising his heel. That's what these lines meant.

> Her child will crush your head
> And you will crush his heel.

In the end the rebel will get his head crushed, Adam said. Instead of conquering, he will be conquered.

While the children were small, that was hard to understand. But they memorized it, and later they saw clearly what the prophecy meant because they saw the war happening in the world around them.

Adam also told his children stories of the garden that God

planted, of plants growing without weeds, of walking with God in the evenings and talking with Him. Sadly, he told about the serpent and the fruit.

When one of the children asked, "Why did you eat that fruit?" it was hard for Adam to answer. Each child liked to think, "I would never have touched the fruit. I would not have eaten it." But in the deepest corner of his heart, when he was really honest, he knew that he would have tasted it too.

When Adam's sons were old enough and it was time for a sacrifice, he let them help kill an animal and prepare it for sacrificing to God. He taught them carefully why this was necessary.

Adam and his children were always learning about the world, too. Every year weeds grew a little worse. They had to chop weeds from their gardens and dig out thorny plants. Plants they cultivated began getting diseases, and they had to learn new sciences in caring for them. Adam could see that the laws of nature he had known in paradise were not operating now. Part of God's holding power was withdrawn, and now a law of decay and death was operating in the the world.

Some people were interested in the science of water. Water came up from the ground in a mist, and in the cool of night fell back to earth as dew, watering pastures and gardens. Under the ground were "great deeps" where much water was stored. In certain places water gushed up from the deeps and became the fountainheads of rivers, which flowed until their water reached the seas, or through some other conduit returned again to underground reservoirs. There, moved about by pressures and earth's inner heat, waters completed their cycle and continually fed the springs at the heads of rivers. The waters above the sky were another study all to themselves.

With work and play and learning, the children grew up. When they were old enough to marry, each young man took a sister or a niece for his wife. In later generations, the men could marry cousins and more distant relatives. Families multiplied and soon they couldn't fit into one house for a family reunion. Many grand children were born, and Adam and Eve still lived. Over a hundred years old, they were young and strong yet, for that was the way of things when the world was new.

As the population grew Adam taught the young fathers that they should teach their children. But Adam himself continued to preach and to teach everybody. Since he was the only father in the world who had walked and talked with God, he felt it was up to him, especially, to pass on the knowledge of God.

The two older sons were making their ways in the world. Cain had settled into being a farmer like Adam, and Abel was a shepherd. Thus when Abel needed grain for his family, he could buy from Cain. And when Cain needed wool or milk or an animal to sacrifice, he could buy from Abel.

Year after year, Cain sold grain and bought sheep, but he was unhappy with this brotherly arrangement. He especially resented it when he had to get a sheep from Abel for a sacrifice. Food that he grew should make just as good a sacrifice as animals, he vainly thought. Why wouldn't God let him offer it?

Cain fed his jealousy by thinking that Abel seemed to be a favorite with God. Abel was a prophet. He learned from God over by the cherubim. He and Adam spent a lot of time talking about God and His promise. They studied the stars. "See the Serpent up there?" they would say when they preached. "See the Virgin who will bear the promised Seed?"

People listened to Abel when he preached about the future of the world and God's plan for it. Even some of Cain's own families liked to hear Abel's preaching.

Cain's jealousy grew and grew, and one day when it was time for a blood sacrifice, he did not get a lamb from Abel. He took food from his garden to offer instead. He pushed away memories of his youth when Adam had taught him what was needed. He could decide what was wrong and what was right just as well as anyone else, and he set his heart to do it his own way this time.

Nearby, Abel offered a sacrifice for his family—a perfect,

Adam's Children

firstborn, young animal from his flock. Fire from between the cherubim came on to the altar and God accepted Abel's offering of meat and fat, but no fire came to burn Cain's.

Cain's face set in hardness and he heard God's voice speaking to him. "Why are you angry? If you do it right you will be accepted, but if you don't, sin crouches at your door."

It was a second chance for Cain, but he did not feel sorry and change his mind. The sin at his door came inside, making his heart harder than before. He did not offer another sacrifice.

Later, by the houses, Abel tried to persuade Cain to obey God. He explained that though Cain was a good farmer, his good works could not satisfy God. He needed faith in the promised Seed, and he needed to show his faith by the right kind of sacrifice.

Cain had heard that preaching before, and he argued. He accused God of having a favorite and he accused Abel of being that favorite. As he shouted at his brother, a terrible idea came into his mind. "Come into my field," he said. "Let us talk in privacy out there." In the field they continued talking until Cain suddenly rose up with one of his garden tools and killed his brother Abel.

Cain had seen the death of animals, but this was the first death of a human. It was shocking even for hard-hearted Cain to see the dead body of his brother lying there. He covered it over with dirt, little thinking that this was part of the war against the promised Seed. The words he had memorized in childhood did not return to him now.

Standing there in the garden, he heard the voice of God. "Where is your brother Abel?" asked the voice. Cain, like his parents in Eden, wouldn't take blame for what he had done. "I don't know," he lied. "Am I my brother's keeper?"

God said, "What have you done? The voice of your brother's blood cries to me from the ground." Then Cain realized that he could not hide his deed from God, but he was not repentant.

God said, "You are cursed from the earth. The ground which opened its mouth to receive your brother's blood that you spilled will not give you good crops anymore. You will be a fugitive and a wanderer in the earth."

This was going to be worse than the curse already on the ground, but it was for Cain alone. Cain said, "That punishment is more than I can bear." His voice sounded sorry now, but it was sorrow not about his deed, only about his punishment. In anguish, he pleaded with God, "You are driving me off my farmland and sending me away from Eden where You are. I will always have to hide, because whoever finds me will kill me."

God heard his plea and said, "Therefore whoever slays Cain shall receive vengeance sevenfold." And He changed Cain's appearance, made him a marked man so that no one finding him would kill him.

Sorrow filled the land of Eden. Those who loved Abel were never going to see him again in this world. They lifted their voices and wept. Some had the tragic duty of finding Abel's body under the soil of the field and digging a more fitting burial place in which to lay it.

Adam preached at the world's first funeral and reminded everyone that God made humans from the ground. "For dust you are, and unto dust shall you return," he recited from memory. To give hope, Adam also recited the promise that someday a child would be born to crush the rebel, finishing sin and death forever. After Adam's speech, they lowered Abel's body into the grave. Shovelfuls of dirt covered it over, and everyone saw what would happen to each of them in time.

Adam and Eve grieved over the loss of Abel, but their hearts pained even more when they thought of Cain. The little boy they had loved, their firstborn son, had grown to be a rebellious murderer. And they were partly responsible because they had started sin in the world.

Cain could not face the people in Eden. While feelings ran high, someone might ignore God's warning of a seven fold punishment and kill him anyway. And people would look with hatred and loathing, he feared. Even before the funeral, Cain hid out. Stealthily he gathered some belongings and his wife and departed from Eden.

5. Cain

With bitter heart, Cain traveled eastward to the land of Nod. He chose a fertile spot and planned to defy the curse of God. God had said the ground would not produce for him and he would be a wanderer in the earth. But he determined to settle down and make his ground produce. After all, he was a good farmer, and he could do it. But at his first location, he soon decided the soil was not good enough for his crops, so he moved to another spot. Not long after, he moved again. And again.

Cain and his wife had a firstborn son whom they named Enoch, to say that they were beginning a new life in this land. Other children were born too, and when they grew up they settled down with farms or flocks. But not Cain. He restlessly wandered from place to place. Grandchildren and great-great grandchildren and more generations were born, and yet Cain lived. When 300 years old, he was still a vigorous man.

Grandfather Cain made sure that everyone knew well the story of how he got away with murder and how God promised a sevenfold punishment upon anyone who killed him. He wasn't so careful with the stories of creation, the garden of Eden, the promised Seed of the woman, and others that Adam and Abel had preached in Eden.

Around firesides at night, fathers told the story of Cain to their children, and throughout the land he was known as the oldest grandfather of their tribe, doomed to wander for the rest of his life. Fathers warned their young sons not to ever get angry with Cain and kill him. They weren't so sure there was a God, but if there were and the story were true, a man's punishment for killing Cain would be seventimes as bad as his crime of murder. Many a little boy shuddered with fear. And some of them, as men, did have cause to be angry with bitter old Cain. But no one would kill him.

As the population grew more numerous, some of the families could do other kinds of work besides farming, and they began living close together in clusters of homes. This gave Cain an idea. As he brooded over his fate, he liked to think that God gave him special protection and no one dared to touch him. But he didn't like the curse that made him a fugitive for all his long life.

He had been unable to change that curse by settling on a farm. But now he had a bold idea that he thought would show God and, moreover, would show all the people that he was not a wanderer. He would be the powerful patriarch over all the people. And he would rule from the biggest city they had ever seen. He chose a name for the city—Enoch, like his son, because the city would mark a new beginning in his life.

Enough people liked the idea that soon it was happening. Somebody surveyed, somebody parceled out real estate, somebody talked merchants into setting up businesses there. Workers erected buildings and laid down streets. Somebody tried to settle quarrels that erupted. People far away heard of the city and moved there. Cain set himself up as mayor, even though some people didn't like that. For a time, while the city was all astir in its newness, it appeared that Cain would change his ways and become a settled citizen.

But trouble flared up, as it always seemed to around Cain, and he walked away from his boldest dream. He left his son Enoch to be mayor and to finish building the city. Ever after that, Cain was known as the eccentric old wandering hermit. People were afraid of him but at the same time were amused at the odd things they heard about him. Most of the stories about Cain were rumor, since no one knew him very well. Those who read history books knew that all the native Easterners, those whose families were not recent immigrants, were descendants of this legendary Cain.

Mayor Enoch, the son of Cain, had grandchildren who were grown and had children of their own. The older generations continued to live, along with the new generations, and the population began to flourish in the East. As their numbers grew, so did their wickedness.

A great-great-grandson of Enoch's was named Lamech, and he, like Cain, was a man whom people told stories about while relaxing by the fireplace at night. Lamech was noted for charming the women. He selected two of the most beautiful women he knew, Adah and Zillah, and married them both.

It wasn't often in the East that anyone talked about the true teachings of God. Only a few people listened to missionaries. Whenever one of them was bold enough to tell Lamech that God setup marriage for a man to have only one wife, Lamech laughed in his face. If he wanted two wives, he would have two wives, and no one was going to take them away.

Lamech could get away with saying anything, because he was building up his own family dynasty of power. His son Tubalcain was famous as the inventor of the science of metallurgy. Lamech helped Tubalcain to acquire mines and build up metalworks. The family grew wealthy as they sold plows, sickles, knives, brass pots, and other inventions that came along in the wake of the new metals Tubalcain was making.

"Why not make a knife with both edges sharp?" asked Lamech one day. It would be just the thing to carry around for protection. It could pierce an enemy easily.

Thus the family who knew the secrets of metallurgy also owned the weapons. They could sell a sword to a man they liked, and they could refuse to sell a sword to a man they did not like. Few people were brave enough to argue with Lamech.

Another son, Jubal, inherited from Lamech an unsurpassed ability in music. Father and son could write poems, set them to music, and sing them. Lamech could see that there was as much power in music as in weapons to influence men, so he encouraged

Jubal and helped him develop his talents. And Jubal became the famous inventor of stringed instruments and wind instruments.

With his new instruments, concerts became better attended than ever. Musicians like Jubal were heroes to the people. Whether they were good men or bad didn't matter, as long as they could sing or play stirring music. Most of their songs told about violence and ungodliness, and people cheered and applauded. Lamech was proud of his son Jubal, who brought so much fame to the family.

In some few homes a mother would say, "No, you can't go to the concert tonight."

"Why not?" the children whined. "All my friends are going."

Most of the mothers couldn't answer that question clearly. But the youth environment seemed worse than when they were young, and they wanted to protect their children from it.

Lamtech's third son, Jabal, was as creative as the others, but he was a wanderer. He invented the tent, a home that herdsmen could carry with them so they could live almost as comfortably as people who lived in the towns. Cattle raising became a big business, and Jabal was famous as the father of the industry. He knew more about it than anybody. Oxen and other strong animals were sold for work. Wool, fleece, hair, leather and other products from animals provided many comforts. This society had long since forgotten God's command to Adam to eat only plant food, so many animals were sold for meat. Cattle raising was almost as lucrative as giving concerts.

Lamech felt secure then. He had wealth and weapons and servants and a large family around him. Enemies could say what they wanted, but they could not touch him.

But in his busy life, he did not notice what was happening close at home. Other men were interested in his beautiful wives, Adah and Zillah. The two women encouraged this because they liked to have men chasing them. One young man in particular was about to take them away from Lamech.

Adam and Eve

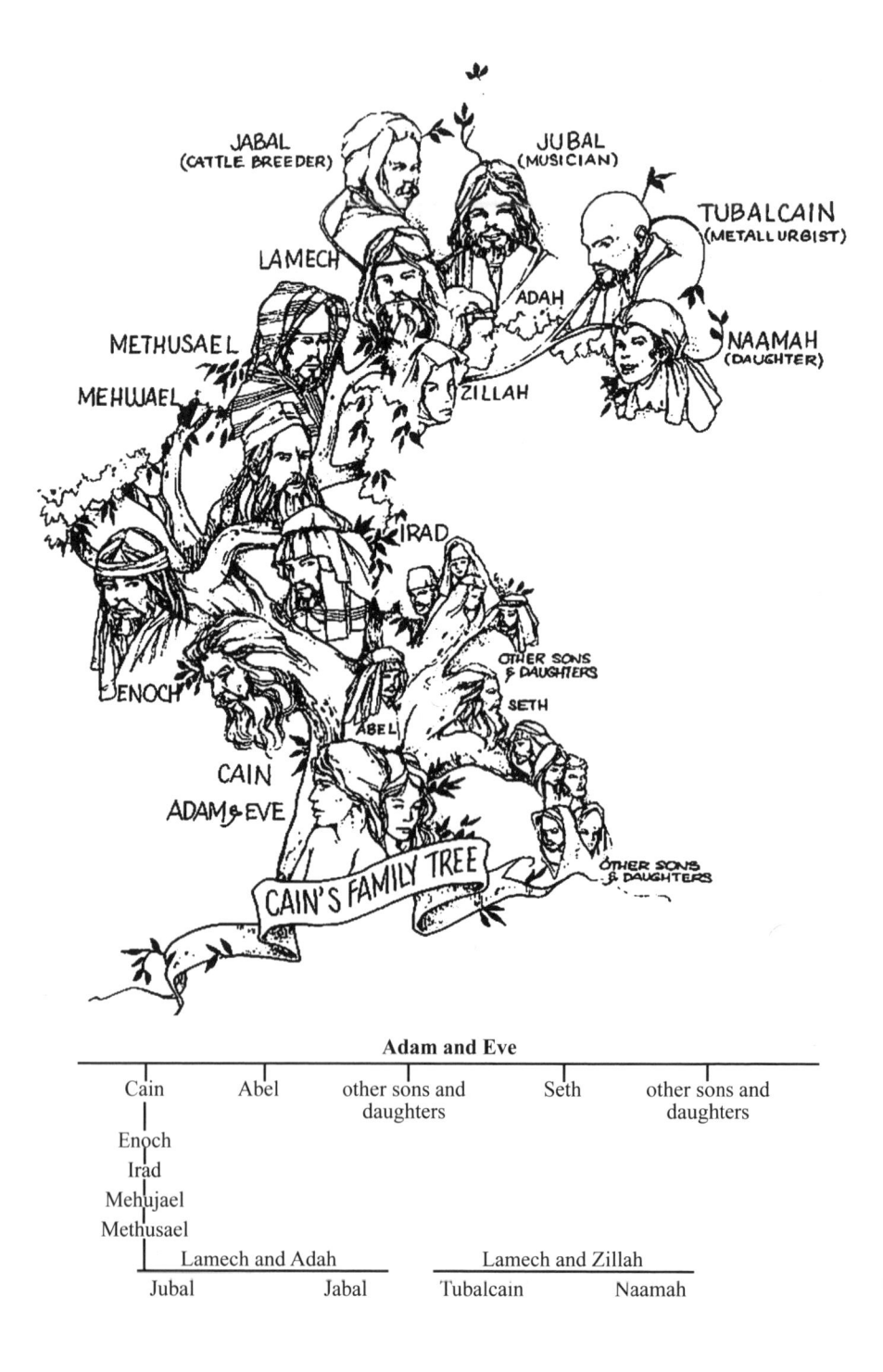

Cain	Abel	other sons and daughters	Seth	other sons and daughters

Cain
 |
Enoch
 |
Irad
 |
Mehujael
 |
Methusael
 |
Lamech and Adah .... Lamech and Zillah
Jubal   Jabal   Tubalcain   Naamah

When Lamech finally heard of the mischief going on, he killed the young man. Strong and wealthy as he was, he didn't worry about what would happen to him; he could continue to live safely on his estate near town. He knew the story of the first murderer and he decided to be bolder yet than Cain. He wouldn't hide the body or hush up the story of his murder.

Lamech was proud of his deed, and yet angry at his wives. In his fury, he wrote a daring song as a warning for them. He wanted them to know that if they ever had any more lovers those would be murdered too. When the song was finished, Lamech came into the house and sang it to his wives.

> Adah and Zillah, hear my voice;
> You wives of Lamech, listen to me.
>
> I have slain a man for wounding me,
> Slain a youth for bruising me.
>
> If Cain be avenged sevenfold,
> Then Lamech, seventy-seven fold.

So proud was Lamech that he let the song be sung at public concerts. Some younger people asked, "Who is Cain?" And older people told them that Cain had murdered his brother and God protected Cain by promising a sevenfold vengeance upon anyone who would kill him.

This made the song understandable to the younger generation. They could now see the point in Lamech promising a seventy-sevenfold vengeance. What a mighty hero was he!

Some concert-goers, in their private thoughts, did not admire the rich, conceited Lamech, but they liked something about the song anyway. While they listened, they felt as strong as a song hero themselves. For a while, this song was the most often requested from musicians who traveled and made it known all over the land. But after a time, newer songs took its place. People forgot Lamech, and other heroes rose to popularity.

Chaos was mounting in those days, and other families built strongholds around themselves as Lamech did. Murder went unpunished, men took more than one wife, plays and other entertainments were full of violence and perversion, and people's lives were becoming just like the entertainments.

Yet people talked about life becoming better all the time. Weren't they making new inventions every year? Weren't they progressing scientifically? Wasn't their literature growing? And their arts?

Some old stargazers told people that all was not well. They said the world was going to be destroyed twice—once by water and once by fire. And the time for water was drawing close.

A few people were interested in the stargazers' words. To think about the end of the world sent little chills of fear up their spines. Is that how the world was going to end? With water drowning it?

Scientists scoffed at that kind of talk. The world had been here for millions of years, they said. And it would be around for millions more. Besides, there was no law of science to account for such a strange end to the world. Right-thinking people didn't have to worry.

But the stargazers persisted. They knew they were right.

6. Writing in the Stars

In Eden, back at the time when Cain fled the country, Eve suffered remorse over the tragedy. She blamed herself for it because she was the first to disobey the Lord God. Alone at night she often cried while thinking about it.

But some of Eve's children helped to comfort her, and now she was expecting another baby. She was still beautiful and young at 130 years of age. She and Adam planned to work especially hard to teach this new child to live in the way of the Lord God instead of the way of Cain.

The baby was born, and it was another boy. Adam knew from God that this boy was the one through whom the promised Seed would come. So Eve was more joyful than she had been in a long time. She cuddled the tiny baby close to her and repeated his name, "Seth . . . Seth." The name meant "appointed one," so it reminded Adam and Eve daily to look forward with hope.

Seth was like his father in many ways. As he grew up, he learned from Adam about the Creator and the creation. He memorized God's book. Its first words were, "In the beginning God created the heavens and the earth." Then it told about the six days in which God created and the seventh day that God made holy because in it He ceased from His work. The book ended with, "This is the account of the heavens and the earth when they were created."

Seth learned from Adam that God not only created the earth and people, He also was going to redeem them, to buy them back from death and corruption. So his Creator studies and creation studies were intertwined, and there seemed no end to what Adam could teach him. No one in the world had so much knowledge as Adam—about plants and animals and stars and people and everything else. Seth continued to study long after he grew up and had a family of his own.

Seth's family lived near Adam and near the cherubim meeting place of God. One day when he was about 105 years old, God removed the flaming lightning bolts and the cherubim. The Tree of Life was gone too, and the Tree of Knowing Good and Evil. Some people said that God took the Tree of Life up into heaven, but they could not prove that. Thorns and thistles had over grown the garden and most people had a fear of it they couldn't explain. Adam and Seth would not allow anyone to homestead that area. They felt it should always be a wilderness uninhabited by man.

At that time, a son was born to Seth, and he named the baby Enos, which was his way of publicly commenting on how frail mortal men were. Men could not see God. They could no longer see the awesome glory of His meeting place. Now they could only call upon His name. This they began to do.

Adam taught people how they should worship and call on God's name. Wherever they might move to, in all their lands, they should gather each Sabbath day and praise the Lord God together. They should read the words that God gave in the creation story and in the prophecies. They should observe an annual festival celebrating the week of creation. They should offer certain sacrifices and remember the coming Redeemer. They should pray, calling upon the name of the Lord.

Adam and Seth and many of the fathers had been teaching their children that God wanted people to fill the earth. So when the children grew up, some of the families began to settle along the rivers that formed from the Eden River which flowed through the old garden and meandered across the gentle landscape. The Eden parted and became four rivers. The first of these four was called the Pison and it flowed around a land which the settlers called

Havilah. They found gold there and precious stones. And they found bdellium, which was good to eat. Havilah was a sandy land with wonderful riches for people who liked to work for them.

The second river was called the Gihon. By following it, people reached a good land that the settlers called Ethiopia.

The third branch was named the Tigris River, and people followed it eastward to the beautiful land of Assyria. The fourth branch was called the Euphrates River. Both the Tigris and Euphrates flowed through valleys with rich farming lands, so many people chose to settle in those areas.

Each time a group prepared to emigrate from Eden, Adam made sure they took with them the words of God about creating the heavens and the earth. "Teach the words to every child," he admonished. "The human race must always remember and worship the Lord God who made them."

Adam and Seth tried to watch over the families. They traveled to new settlements and helped them properly set up their worship and obey God. On their visits they taught more about God and the prophecies. To help people remember, they would point to the sky and say, "See that Serpent up there in the stars? Let him remind you of the enemy you must resist. And remember, at the end times of history the Serpent will be crushed by the Redeemer." The two fathers continually urged people to be faithful to God.

The population continued to grow and settle farther out, so more teachers and preachers helped Adam. And Adam told the fathers they must teach their own families. They must help to pass God's message from generation to generation. Some fathers did this job faithfully, and others did not.

Seth faithfully taught his children, and many of his sons and grandsons did also. For a while, then, the Sethites were known as a godly tribe. It was better to live in Eden and its settlements than to live in Nod with the Cainites. There was less violence and less wickedness of all kinds. More people loved God.

But even in Eden some children had rebellious hearts. When

they became fathers they didn't teach their families as they should, so after a few generations, life in their part of the world began to parallel life in Nod.

Adam grieved at the way the world was going. At 600 years of age he still preached righteousness, but too many people were unrighteous. He could see that knowledge of God was growing dim in the world. People who wanted to know could listen to and talk to the only living man who had walked and talked with God, but what would happen after he died? To help future generations, he wrote a book about God.

He also spent much time with Seth studying and preaching from the book God had written in the sky. If people could read those signs in the starry heavens, they would never be without God's message. Night after night the knowledge of God shone upon the whole world. They must teach people how to read it.

The promised Redeemer could be seen up there, triumphant even while the Serpent was crushing His heel, because though He must first die, He would rise again, triumphant over death. It took many pictures to say all the wonderful things that people needed to know about the Redeemer, so another picture showed Him as the atonement and as the Lamb, the perfect sacrifice which would finally pay for sins, as the present sacrifices could not. Another showed Him as the coming Judge and King to rule over all the earth. Still another showed him as the Shepherd keeping His flocks safe in the fold.

So exciting were these studies that a school of followers came to Eden to learn from Adam and Seth. After a man had learned the basics, Adam would send him back home or to another country as a missionary. "Go tell what you know about God," he encouraged every student.

At this time, it happened that Seth's great-great-grandson Jared and his wife were expecting a new child. "The child will have special work to do for God," announced Seth. "You must train him well."

Writing in the Stars

When the baby arrived, the parents joyfully dedicated him to the Lord God. They named him Enoch. Their distant Uncle Enoch over in the land of Nod had a notorious reputation, but they knew it would be different with this Enoch.

As soon as the child was old enough, Jared brought him to Adam and Seth to learn from them how to serve the Lord God. Thus from his childhood, Enoch came to know some matters that Seth had not known until he was a couple hundred years old. He was especially interested in astronomy, and having such an early start it became apparent that he would be able to develop this kind of knowledge farther than any other person could. Adam and Seth trained him to do this. It also became apparent that Enoch was chosen by God to be a prophet.

The young astronomer worked with the old astronomers for almost 300 years. What wonderful and rich studies they had! Adam and Seth had laid the groundwork and Enoch, building on their knowledge, worked out a total system for understanding the heavens. He became famous as the inventor of the system of astronomy. The signs and seasons and days and years could now be known by anyone willing to study them. The mansions for the moon and the tabernacle for the sun were charted in their marvelous patterns. The fixed stars, the wandering stars, the sun and the moon proclaimed the seasons of God's plan for mankind. Some men read the signs and many ignored them; yet day after day and night after night their message went out to all the world. Preachers of righteousness could travel anywhere and point out to men the writing in the stars.

Sometimes Enoch preached about the sign of the Bull in the stars. Most people had learned how to outline the powerful Bull in their imaginations. They knew the bright star, The Follower, in his eye, and The Butting One at the tip of his horn, and others. At times the bull was called Reem, because he was so powerful. At other times he had the special name Shur, which meant coming and ruling. That's the name Enoch liked to use.

"See how he is rushing," Enoch would say, "with his horns lowered ready to pierce anything in his way. He shows us that the heavenly Judge will push down his enemies all over the earth. He will punish the world for their evil and the wicked for their sins.

"And see the cluster of stars on his shoulder and the cluster on his face," Enoch would continue. Those stars, he explained, stood for ten thousands of people belonging to the ruler. And he quoted a prophecy which God had given him.

> Behold the Lord comes with ten thousands of his holy ones to execute judgment upon all, and to convince all that are ungodly among them of all their ungodly deeds which they have ungodly committed, and of all their hard speeches which ungodly sinners have spoken against him.

The words were thrilling to those who believed them. They liked to picture the strong Bull and themselves riding upon it. Yes, even they might come riding with the Judge, and the world would then be a better place in which to live, perhaps a paradise again.

But people living ungodly lives were angered to hear Enoch say the strong word *ungodly* so often.

But Enoch did not need to be a popular speaker. In his heart he knew his words were right. God was pleased with him even if men were not. Enoch wrote the words in a book of prophecies. If people in his generation wouldn't listen, at least in future generations some people would read the words and turn to God. Then they could be among the ten thousands coming with the Judge instead of among those who would suffer the judgment.

One day Enoch prophesied that there would be a judgment sooner than the one in which the Lord comes to earth. It would destroy the world by water. Some followers who believed Enoch said, "We must build a monument that will outlast the water. We must write God's message in a way that can be read by mankind after the water judgment."

THE BUTTING ONE

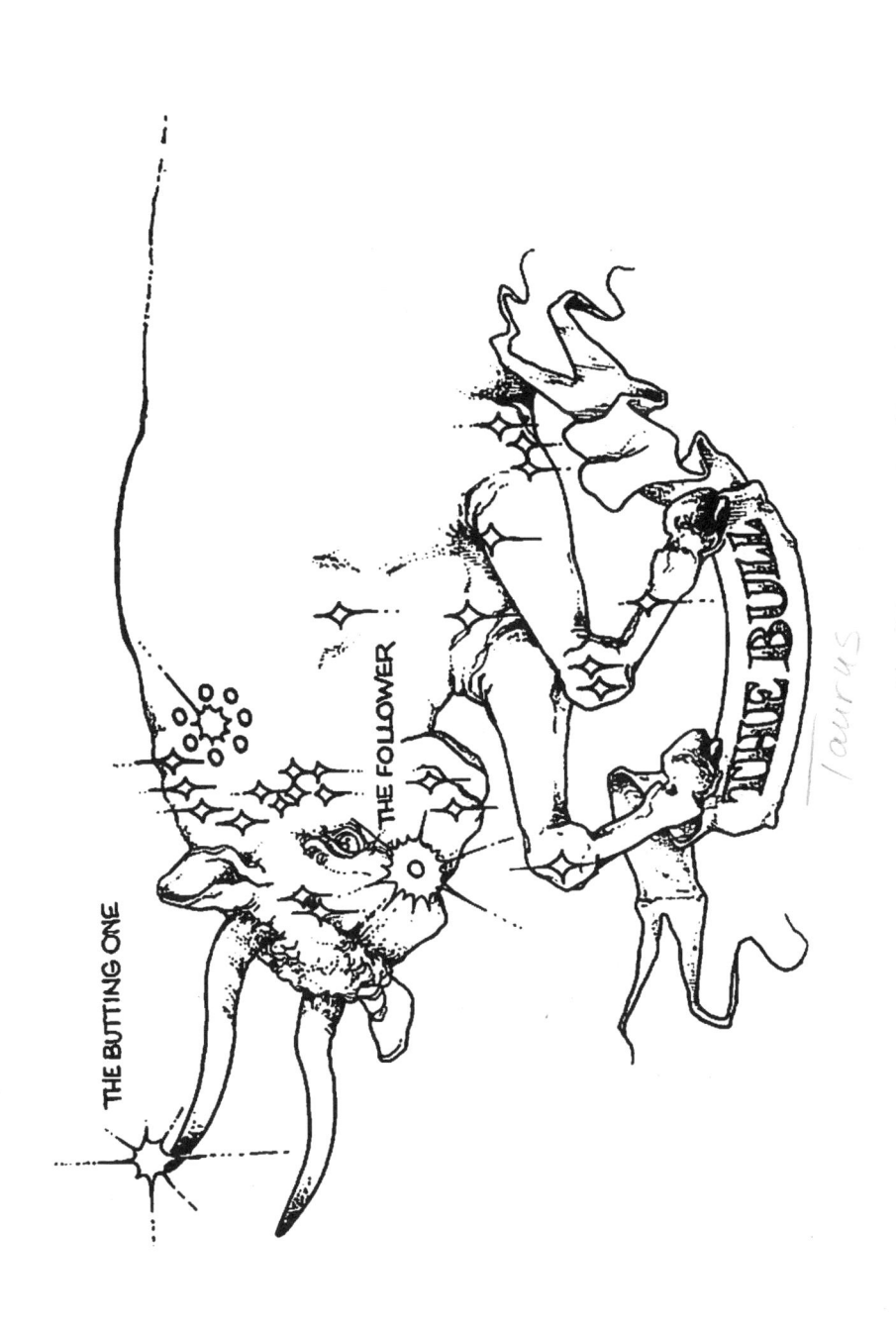

THE FOLLOWER

THE BULL

Taurus

Other believers said, "No, we must spend our time evangelizing. If people turn to God, then it may be that God will withhold the judgment."

Nobody won the argument. Some spent their time evangelizing and others raised money and organized workers for the monument. They built it of brick, as strong as their technology could achieve, and they inscribed God's words and the history of their times. Men in after times would want to know.

"It's not strong enough," some people objected. "Raging water can eat away our structure and weaken it. At least it will obscure the inscription."

So other men built another monument, this time of stone. Certain workers, unbeknown to the others, hid a time capsule within the monument. And on the outside, engravers put their messages in stone for all to see. Then they felt they had done what they could to help survivors. Let the water judgment come.

7. The Preachers

Adam was over 900 years old and knew that he was soon to die. He checked over a history book in which he told of the garden, the geography of Eden and its neighbors, the story of his sin including the curses and the wonderful promise, and the story of Cain and Abel. He also had included the history of Cain's descendants, the ones he obtained news of when someone traveled to or from the eastern lands. So the book told of Cain's city, of the extraordinary inventions in that land, and of Lamech's song about the brazen murder of a young man.

"Maybe you should omit the Lamech story," someone suggested. "No," said Adam. "It shows the true condition of men's hearts at this time in history."

He left the Lamech story in the book, but finishing on a happier tone, he wrote that Eve bore Seth who was God's appointed one. And to Seth was born Enos, and in his time men began to call upon the name of the Lord. That was a good place to end. Adam signed off his history with the words:

This is the written account of Adam.

There also was the unfinished record that he and Seth were keeping of the descendants in Seth's line. They both knew how important it would be for future generations, since the Redeemer was to come through Seth's line. They had recorded births, but no deaths yet. The list included Adam, Seth, Enos, Cainan, Mahalaleel, Jared, Enoch, Methuselah, and Lamech. This Lamech, the grandson of Enoch, was a different kind of man from his distant cousin Lamech in Nod. Adam was happy for that.

Adam died at the age of 930 years. He had lived through all the history of the world. Many descendants from Eden and other lands mourned the loss of their oldest patriarch. They tenderly laid him in the ground and Seth quoted, "For dust you are, and unto dust shall you return." Then he quoted happier prophecies that Adam had taught, about the Redeemer.

The mourners remembered Adam's voice, which could no longer proclaim those words, and they realized how the seasons of mankind roll onward. The world would never be the same without Adam.

Seth was now the head preacher of righteousness, and he continued Adam's work. Enos preached too, and other descendants. But by Enoch's generation, the seventh from Adam, most of the world's population had gone the way of Cain and only a few still listened to the preachers. The preachers did not say so much in these days about the coming Redeemer and the loving Shepherd. More and more they preached about the impending judgment.

Enoch's son had the long name Methuselah, which meant "when he dies, judgment." Enoch had put this prophecy of God into his son's name at birth, and it was understood in all lands, wherever people saw or heard of Methuselah. Now, in the year of Adam's death, he was 243 years old. He had learned from his father Enoch and studied in the school of Adam and Seth. He was a preacher too.

Neighbors had watched the boy grow up, and he didn't die. His hundredth birthday passed, and his two hundredth birthday passed, and like most everyone else he still had a long life ahead of him. Those who worried at first over the prophecy in Methuselah's name hardened their hearts with each year that went by. Now they scoffed with the others, "What gloom and doomers in Enoch's family! Always trying to tell us about judgment."

Enoch continued to work on his system of astronomy. He knew exactly the road through the stars which the sun traveled on its ecliptic each year. And he worked out calculations for the paths of the moon and the wandering stars. Those five wandering stars which the eye could see, along with the sun and moon, made seven altogether that moved in the sky. Enoch could read signs so well that these movements were always giving him more information about what God was going to do in the world.

Sometimes the paths of two wandering stars converged and they appeared from earth to be as one star. Sometimes a wanderer converged with a fixed star, and since Enoch knew the names of so many stars he could read messages in these wanderings. Seth described to him the unusual state of the heavens on the night Enoch was born. The astronomers were excited then and were not surprised later when Enoch became a prophet. They were waiting to see what else God would do with this remarkable man who was always studying the stars and telling about God.

Enoch calculated the paths of the wanderers. He became especially interested in the largest wanderer, the King Star, and was startled one day to discover some extraordinary future events. Three times, one right after another, the King Star would come into conjunction with the bright Little King Star in the Lion. During that same time the King would also meet twice with the brightest wanderer, that bright and morning star. In all, four of the wanderers would move into the sign of the Lion. He studied these and other movements in the heavens and began to realize that he was reading an announcement of the Redeemer himself—Him whose star shall come and whose scepter shall arise.

That time was about 3000 years into the future, and Enoch did not know where or among what people the Redeemer might come. But astronomers of those days, if they read these announcements and then looked for the new star—His star—they could find and identify Him—the Seed promised to Adam, the Great King that the world needed.

Enoch wrote it in his book and he told some of the astronomers and preachers. Hardly anyone else was interested.

For over 300 years Enoch prophesied and preached and studied the stars. Other preachers admired his life and tried to live like him. They wondered sometimes if Enoch was almost like Adam when he walked with God in the garden of Eden.

But leaders in the cities came to hate the very name Enoch. Through the years, their wickedness grew worse until they could not tolerate Enoch's preaching of judgment. It interfered too much with the buying and selling of intoxicating substances and with other activities that gave leaders their power over other people.

One day Enoch said he must go to the cities downriver from where he lived. He began to walk, and young men from the preachers' school accompanied him. As they approached the first city, preachers came out to meet them and begged Enoch not to enter their city. It was too dangerous for him, they said. And they asked the young men, "Don't you know that today the Lord God will take your master from you?" The young men knew but did not want to talk about it.

Enoch and his young men walked on, and the city preachers followed from afar. They approached the next city and a group of preachers came out to meet them. They begged Enoch not to enter their city, and they asked the young men, "Don't you know that today the Lord God will take your master from you?" The young men would not talk about it.

Enoch and the young men walked on, and the preachers watched from atop a hill beside the river valley. Then all at once Enoch was not walking with the men. Seventy witnesses saw that Enoch was not, and they knew that the Lord God had taken him.

When this news reached the cities, it spread like wildfire and the leaders discussed how they could stop it. "It is only that he fell into the river and drowned," said one. They sent out crews to drag the river for Enoch's body, but they could not prove that he had drowned.

The Preachers 49

"Perhaps the preachers hid him in the hills," suggested another. They sent out search parties, but they could not prove that Enoch was hiding in the hills.

The leaders made some of the preachers to understand that if they wanted to live in the cities they must say that God had sent judgment on Enoch for thinking he was so good. Worried and scared people listened to the new preaching about judgment, and they felt better.

In more distant towns people thought up other ideas. Was the missionary money missing too? Someone should check on that. Did Enoch sneak away to another land? He was a strange man, you know, and he might do that to make people think God took him.

Some parents told their children that Enoch went up to the stars and if they would look up there on a dark night they could see him.

Family members and friends gathered, some traveling from distant places. They worshiped the Lord God who had power to take Enoch to heaven without dying. And they talked about Enoch and his faithful life. Preachers among them reminded people of Enoch's prophecies, and they admonished each other to remain faithful in their society, which had all but forgotten the Creator.

Methuselah was now 300 years old, and this sudden taking of Enoch reminded the whole family that God could also suddenly take Methuselah in death. Any year now, any day, the judgment could come.

Seth brought to the family reunion his record of the Seed line. It still listed births down to Lamech and it had only one death so far—Adam's. What should they say now about Enoch? They talked it over, and Seth wrote:

> Enoch lived 60 and 5 years and begat Methuselah:
> And Enoch walked with God after he begat Methuselah
> 300 years, and begat sons and daughters:
> And all the days of Enoch were 360 and 5 years:

And Enoch walked with God:
And he was not; for God took him.

Some men added this to family histories they were keeping, and Seth turned over his record to Methuselah. Everyone felt the seriousness of this occasion. Their kinsman Enoch had preached so often of judgment coming upon the world, and now God had ended Enoch's preaching, but in so remarkable a way that it affirmed the truth of his words.

Methuselah, standing in their midst, was a living legacy from Enoch. As long as he lived, they could preach righteousness and truth and perhaps save some people from destruction. When he died, their time would be up, as Enoch's now was. They all realized they may not meet again. Their lives were like a vapor. Only Methuselah had assurance of living until the time of judgment. He would know what to do with the records.

So Seth handed into his keeping all the important books: the book of God, the books of Adam, and the unfinished genealogy. Methuselah also took into his care his father's books of prophecy and astronomy.

The families parted solemnly, calling upon the name of God that He might have mercy on them, forgive their sins, and preserve them from the coming judgment. They all returned to their estates and towns with renewed resolve to warn neighbors, if any would listen, and to teach their children well.

Fifty-five years later Seth died, at the age of 912. Some of the family once again gathered, and they buried him lovingly, as they had Adam. Enoch was gone, and now Seth. The words of these preachers no longer thundered in the land, nor were they reported from city to city. There was less fear of God than ever before.

At that time another baby was born into the preacher family, a little son of Lamech, who was the son of Methuselah. This made the baby the tenth generation in the Seed line, and Lamech received word from God that the child would provide salvation from the

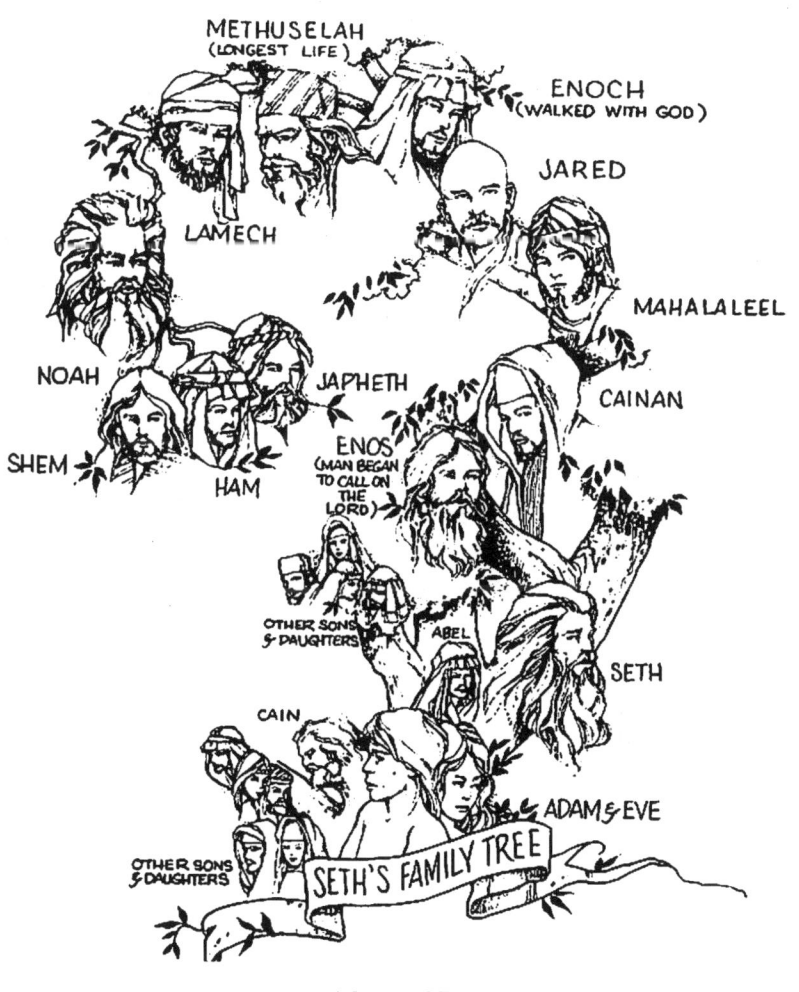

		Adam and Eve		
Cain	Abel	other sons and daughters	Seth	other sons and daughters
			Enos	
			Cainan	
			Mahalaleel	
			Jared	
			Enoch	
			Methuselah	
			Lamech	
			Noah	
		Japheth	Shem	Ham

coming judgment. He would bring rest and comfort to the people of God. So Lamech named him Comfort, or Noah.

The tired and degenerate society around him paid no attention to this new warning from God that the judgment was near. Their minds had no room for thoughts like that.

Noah grew up learning from the books and prophecies. Like those before him, he memorized God's account of creating the heavens and the earth. He memorized the promise and other parts of the writings of Adam, Seth and Enoch. He often wished he could have talked with Adam, the man who talked with God. But he had to content himself with hearing about Adam from his grandfather Methuselah and his father Lamech. He also read Adam's books, which was almost as good as talking with him.

Lamech and Methuselah realized anew how important were the books, and they tried to impress this on Noah. "Generations after you will need them more than ever," they said. "People can't hear Adam talk about God, they can't hear Enoch prophesy, they can't figure out by themselves the true story of the beginnings. So you must preserve these books."

Noah learned, also, about the writing in the stars. He studied Enoch's astronomy books. Together with his father and grandfather, they talked about the wisdom of Enoch and Adam and Seth. And it always seemed that they understood less than those patriarchs.

This made them sad. Was the human race losing knowledge? Was this the destiny for them and their children?

8. Noah

A terrible new epidemic of sin infected society. It started with people being curious about spirit beings. Emptied of God as their minds were, they were vulnerable to the man-hating angels. Demons, the preachers called them.

What began in secret meetings with a few people in dark rooms now became an open practice. People all over the lands were contacting demons, and they bragged about it. They wrote stories and plays about it. Those who had never seen a demon yearned for the day they would. Even children and youth got interested. It was blood-chilling to imagine the day they might see one of those fearful beings, and yet they were drawn by a fascination for evil. They all wanted to be initiated into the experiences their heroes and heroines were having.

Such was the world when angels began to appear in human form. The first rumors were that a famous singer married one of them. Then other beautiful women followed, the wealthy and powerful, those who could have anything on earth that they wanted. Some who were in high society sought their unions secretly, others wanted their actions to be known and talked about. They wanted friends to be jealous.

Scientific and highly educated people showed no understanding of what was taking place. Some thought the people were simply superstitious. Others thought there was truth in the reports, but then they argued about who the beings could be. Life from another world, perhaps? Some race of beings who had evolved farther than man?

The women bore children who grew to unusual size. They were strong and brutish. As their numbers rapidly increased, the world saw a population explosion. Violent gangs fought on city streets and roamed the countryside, raiding estates. People locked their doors, and they added iron bars to their windows. At country estates they reinforced their walls and set armed guards to watch by day and by night.

In spite of all they could do, no one was safe. People worshiped the evil gods with elaborate and fearful ceremonies. Humans were sacrificed in public squares, and on hilltops, from where the fires and frenzied dancing could be seen for miles around.

On any particular night in any particular city a number of people were assaulted and murdered. Common people spent their money on beer and whiskey and prostitutes, while the wealthy spent theirs on wine and luxuries and all the sins they could invent. Richly gowned ladies and their lordly escorts thronged the theaters and concert halls, for music and poetry and literature soothed their minds and filled them with notions of how high and noble their society was becoming. Rowdier crowds jammed into sports arenas and exulted in the violent and bloody spectacle of man's strength and skill.

This was the world Noah lived in. Only Methuselah and Lamech remained of his ancestors. The older ones had died, and just three preachers remained. They were very discouraged. The rebel angels were waging total war, and the preachers worked continuously at bolstering each other's faith lest they slip into believing that the old serpent might win. When would the peace come, the comfort that God promised?

Centuries passed. The world became still more corrupt, and Noah tried to preach truth.

At last, when Noah was 480 years old, the preachers heard from God again. "My spirit shall not always strive with man," He said. "Yet his days shall be 100 and 20 years."

One hundred twenty years! Now Methuselah knew how long he would live. Noah knew the time of the judgment. Both of them, as well as Lamech, renewed their efforts to warn people. But the world seemed beyond saving. Even Noah's own family was drawn into the unbelief and wickedness.

At age 500, Noah had a new son, Japheth, followed by two more sons, Shem and Ham. Shem was chosen for the Seed line. Noah determined to shelter all three sons from the schooling and other influences of society and to raise them for the Lord God. He kept them very close to home.

One day God spoke directly to Noah about coming judgment.

> The end of all flesh is come before me; for the earth is filled with violence through them; and behold, I will destroy them with the earth.

It was going to be the water judgment, God told Noah. A cataclysm of water would destroy every living thing upon the earth. But Noah was to build a boat, an ark huge enough for him and his wife and his sons and the wives they would have, for two of every kind of land animal and fowl, and for food for them all.

God gave Noah exact specifications for building the ark. It was to be larger than any boat ever built, three stories high, with many rooms and stalls and nests, and with a window running around the top just under the roof. It would need particular dimensions in order to withstand surging tides and storms such as the world had never seen. It should be made from a certain material called gopher wood, and be waterproofed with resin.

Noah's experience at managing his own wealth and businesses were going to help him now. He set about immediately to plan the operation. He first sold some assets, both to raise money for materials and to free his time for the new job of boat building.

He arranged for more hardwood timber to be delivered over the next few decades than the lumber company had ever supplied to a single job. No one could provide enough resin of the kind and quality he needed, so Noah set up his own resin company. He hired knowledgeable men to buy forest land and to plant the kind of trees necessary, so that resin would be available when the time came to put a covering on the boat. Some men experimented with synthetic resin; others designed and manufactured new tools for various special tasks. No one had done a job quite like this before and it required careful engineering and good technology.

Even with prudent planning, things often went wrong. Suppliers were undependable, sub-contractors were dishonest, craftsmen were not as skilled as they used to be. Problems plagued Noah at every stage of construction.

Noah put his growing boys to work on some of the projects. It was good training for them and it would help keep them away from evil companions and their ideas. Japheth developed into an excellent planner and trouble-shooter, Ham was the finest craftsman, and Shem preferred to research possible causes for the water catastrophe that was coming.

Shem's brothers sometimes derided him for not being more help on the boat, but his father understood. Noah could see that Shem took after Enoch and Seth. Noah had never known these two ancestors personally, since Enoch had gone to heaven and Seth had died shortly before Noah was born. But all his life Noah had heard almost as much about these two ancestors as about the first one, Adam. The vast learning of Seth and the deep spirituality of Enoch were treasured in the family. Noah was proud to have a son who seemed to inherit their traits.

Shem studied the heavens and the earth in his search for an explanation of the coming cataclysm. Sometimes he thought it might have an astral cause. A comet or a planet, if it came too close, could exert such a pull upon the earth that all kinds of havoc would ensue, both with the earth and with the other astral body. He searched Enoch's astronomy writings and prophecies for any clue he might find there.

Sometimes he wondered if a simpler cause, on the earth

only, might be the answer. For instance, if the earth's inner heat increased—and he had a couple of ideas about how that might happen—too much pressure could build up in the underground water system. Reservoirs would collapse and eruptions would occur. What sort of material would be forced upward in an eruption? Would some of the material getting into the upper atmosphere cause the water up there to fall to earth? That seemed a good possibility to Shem. With both the underground water and the upper water involved, there was more than enough to bring about the end of the world. Shem tried to explain his theory to his brothers and his parents.

Those speculations were interesting, but more practical was Shem's study of animals. How many big stalls and how many small ones would be needed on the ark? Shem tried to get a count. He was personally acquainted with many of the animals and birds from the fields and forests and farms around home, but he certainly didn't know them all. Adam's writings on the created beings helped him catalog the animals and estimate the kinds and amounts of food they would need.

Noah and his wife were on the lookout for girls who would make suitable wives for their sons. Which girls would believe God's word and be willing to enter the ark with them when the time came? They encouraged the daughters of certain neighbors to spend time at their house. And they took interest in the daughters of servants in their own household. Noah taught the girls, and his wife let them help with her work.

In time, Noah selected wives and his three sons were married. The girls' parents laughed with everyone else about Noah's giant boat project, but they were not reluctant to let their daughters marry into such a wealthy family.

Year after year, the boat-building continued. Noah's employees were thankful for the steady work and the fair pay, but they didn't believe in the project itself. A boat that large was not needed anywhere in the world. It would be impossible to move it to water.

And, even if it were in the water, it lacked a means of navigation. They didn't believe the terrifying cataclysm Noah kept talking about could happen. Noah was quite smart about a lot of things, but he was insane to talk about such a catastrophe.

While eating their lunches all the workmen discussed and agreed on these matters. The few who privately worried that Noah might be right, did not have the courage to speak up.

Noah's father and grandfather were his strongest supporters through all those years. But the day came when Lamech died, and grandfather Methuselah was Noah's only remaining ancestor.

Methuselah had now lived longer than anyone in the records he was keeping. Seth had recorded most of the births, and every century or so Methuselah had recorded the age of death after a name. So far, his grandfather Jared had lived the longest—962 years. But while he had the book out to record Lamech's death, he noted that his own age was now greater even than Jared's. That should be a message to people, he thought. It was as though God was giving people extra time to repent and call upon the name of the Lord. But no one did. Those who believed Enoch's prophecies and other words of God had all passed on from this world. Methuselah was forced to agree with God that it was time for judgment.

He gave the books to Noah. "I will not live much longer," he said, and he talked earnestly with Noah, trying to give him wisdom and courage for the awesome responsibility ahead.

Noah needed that support. If all flesh was to be destroyed, he alone, with his family, would be starting things up again. He thought back through history to the time of Adam. Did Adam have fears such as he was having now? No, he decided. It wasn't the same with Adam. And Adam was a great man, while he was just Noah. The boat would soon be finished. Was he ready for what was about to happen?

9. The Year of 1656

The New Year of 1656 arrived. The world celebrated and many deaths occurred on that wild night, some due to accidents and some to murders. Like Lamech the Cainite, murderers could brag and become heroes.

In lands which still used the original calendar, people had lost the meaning that this was now 1656 years from the creation of the world. A few textbooks taught that the years were numbered from the beginning of the dynasty of Adam in Eden, but others omitted even that information because writers were no longer sure it was true, and they didn't think it was important anyway. Some lands had another calendar that originated in Nod, so the numbering was different, but even Nod's astronomers wouldn't let them change the start of the year. It irritated some of the city leaders that astronomers were so slow to accept modern ideas.

While the world celebrated, Methuselah lay on his deathbed. For a time he hung on to life, and he passed his 969th birthday. Noah hardly left his side. The two men talked about the Lord God, the Creator of heaven and earth. They talked about God's promises and the Redeemer to come. In these conversations Noah found comfort and strength. He who was supposed to bring comfort was leaning upon another for the comfort he needed.

In a few weeks, Methuselah died. He was buried and mourned by the family and a few other people who showed respect for the old man. Newsmen paid no attention to this portentious death. They were all occupied with mighty heroes of combat, famous entertainers, the doings of socialites, and other topics they knew would interest the public.

After Methuselah's funeral, Noah sat down with the genealogical record and wrote in Methuselah's age. Then, feeling a heavy burden upon his shoulders, he continued writing. In a few words he told of the terrible wickedness that had come upon the earth because of mankind's communion with demons. In a few more words he told that God was grieved and was going to destroy every living thing upon the earth. He finished his writing with these words.

> But Noah found grace in the eyes of the Lord. This is the written account of Noah.

He closed the book. In his heart he was finished with this world. The boat was ready. He was ready. He had done all that God had told him to do. He carried the genealogy and the other family books onto the boat and stored them carefully. This was too important to trust to anyone else. God's book about creation was there, and Adam's books, Enoch's prophecies and astronomy writings, some praise poetry and wisdom literature from other sons of Seth, and the family genealogy.

No other books seemed to matter. Popular poetry and literature? He couldn't bear to think of them. Books about the trades and crafts? No, let them perish with their world. Science? No, they were filled with lies about the origin of life and other matters. Noah suddenly felt weary of books. He couldn't consider any more of them. He went outside and walked around the boat, inspecting its coating of resin as he went.

The next day the Lord spoke to Noah. "Come into the ark, you and your family, for I have seen that you are righteous before me in this generation." The Lord told him to board clean beasts by sevens and unclean beasts by two, male and female, and the birds also.

There were only seven days left, the Lord told Noah, and

then He would cause it to rain upon the earth forty days and forty nights. Every living substance, of plants and animals and people, would be destroyed from the face of the earth.

Animals had been acting strangely for days, and some were clustered around Noah's boat eating ravenously from his piles of food. As Noah and his sons went out this morning, more animals were arriving from all directions. Those who had eaten their fill could be docilely guided onto the boat, each into a stall or nest just its size, and once there they promptly went to sleep.

Noah was full of energy again, trying to keep things going smoothly with this task of herding animals. The craftsmen had all been let go when the boat was finished, so Noah and his sons were doing the work. Their wives came out to help too.

Word quickly spread to nearby towns. The story of Noah and his boat was an old one, but on this day it had a new twist. "Have you heard the latest in the saga of the ark? Today the whole family's out there loading animals."

"Loading animals? What a laugh! Let's go watch."

The curious came. Noah could not count the times he had preached to such crowds, but today he had his hands full with the animals. Should he stop and preach? Something of his feelings from the previous evening came over him. He was through with this world. He had agonized often for the people, and they wouldn't listen. Is this how God felt? God had named just eight people to go aboard the boat. Was there no hope now for anyone else?

After debating with himself, Noah took time to explain that God was bringing the animals. "These animals know more than you," he said. "Judgment is coming in seven days. Water will fall from the sky for forty days and forty nights. Every living substance, of plants and animals and people, will be destroyed from the face of the earth." There! He had given them the newest words from God. He continued, from long habit, to tell them how to repent and call upon the name of the Lord.

The people had had much practice at closing their hearts to the

Lord, so they didn't give a thought to Noah's entreaties to repent. But falling water from the sky—that gave them something to laugh about. Everybody knew that water came up from the ground, not down from the sky. The laws of hydrology had been working for eons, and they could be trusted to continue working just as regularly in the future. Yes, Noah had gone mad.

In the next few days more curious people came to watch. Noah felt that proceeding with the job of loading animals was the best kind of preaching he could do in these last days. This way, people ought to see that he really believed God's words. But then, on the other hand, they should have seen it during the past hundred years or so.

The last of the food for animals and people was loaded. Seed corn, seed barley, and other such necessities were all checked over to see if anything had been forgotten. The ladies saw that their household treasures were taken on board. Long before this week they had decided what would be useful to have on the boat and afterward, and what would simply be excess baggage. So there were few regrets about leaving possessions behind. The men stowed away tools they wanted.

All this time most of the animals remained in a dormant condition that surprised everybody. Their fat stomachs were still full of food, and they slept or just looked at people through slits in their eyes. Even the curious onlookers were amazed at their behavior.

<u>On the seventh day Noah went into the boat, along with his wife and his sons and his sons' wives.</u> Noah debated again. Should he just walk out of sight, or should he say some last words to the people outside? He stood in the doorway for a moment, then he faced the people, quoted one of the old prophecies about the Redeemer, and disappeared into the dark interior.

The door lifted and shut seemingly by itself. Observers looked at each other quizzically. What kind of magic was this? There was nothing more to watch, so they turned toward their homes, pulling their cloaks tightly around them. Was that ominous feeling in the air just in their imaginations because they had been watching so strange a sight? Or was it real?

10. The Great Flood

Some people did not even reach their homes before terror engulfed them. The ground began shaking under them. Geysers of water shot upwards for hundreds of feet. Rivers rapidly over flowed. The sky grew dark, and rain began pouring down.

Inside the boat, Noah's family heard rumblings and felt quakings, and fear came into their hearts too. Memories from the years of planning and work flashed through their minds. Ham remembered times when he had wanted to quit. Others remembered when this day seemed unreal and far in the future, but now it was here. Had they built the boat right? Was it strong and water tight? Would it float? What was happening to people outside the boat? They imagined, with a tinge of satisfaction, the fear in leaders and in some of the worst people they knew. They worried about people who hadn't seemed so bad as others. What were they thinking now?

Silently they listened to the roaring outside, each person keeping his fears to himself. At length Noah said, "We need not be afraid. Remember that God told me a hundred years ago to build this ark. Remember that God told us it was time to enter. He brought the animals, and He shut the door. God would not lead us through all these preparations and then abandon us now."

Noah's quiet voice exuded confidence, and the tense faces around him relaxed slightly. He continued talking, reminding his family of memorable events during the construction years, of problems and successes and blunders. Soon the others contributed memories of humorous incidents, and a couple of times family members laughed a little.

After a time, less apprehensive than before, some felt brave enough to climb up to the window level and look out. They followed Japheth and observed from the same location. What they saw were frighteningly dark skies and water pounding upon the boat and its surroundings. Because of darkness and water they could not see far, so individuals moved to various locations along the window, which ran all the way around the boat. When someone shouted, "Look, I see a column of water shooting like a fountain up to the sky," the others hurried to that side so they could see it too.

Ham considered the window construction. How much water might come in? Not much, it seemed. Water shed from the roof above the window onto the lower roof and ran off its slope in sheets. Shem sifted through his theories about the catastrophe and tried to figure out what was actually happening. How would he write up these events in a history book? Japheth checked some of the animals, and only a few needed comforting. Most were more soundly asleep than before. Later he went to see if the women needed help getting out some food for dinner.

That night everyone lay awake for a long time listening to the unfamiliar sounds of rain and earthquake, but eventually exhaustion overtook them one by one and they fell asleep. After a couple of days they adjusted to the noise and turbulence, and they began to think about keeping a diary of events and organizing their eating and working schedules. They tried to ignore the world outside.

One day they felt a different kind of movement of the boat, not like an earthquake, but gentler and more rhythmical. "We're floating!" someone exclaimed. After a moment of fear about the integrity of the boat, almost everyone showed excitement. Their decades of construction, their lifetime of devotion to the project, their difficulties and quarrels and problem solving, all were wrapped up now in a few moments of exultation. "We did it! It's seaworthy!"

Ham quietly went to the lowest level to check for leaks. He had been doing this for several days without mentioning it to anyone. He found no water. Some of the others climbed up to the window level and looked out. They could not peer down the sides of the huge hull because the window opening was too far from the outside edge, running as it did along the center from bow to stern. Rain was still pouring down and interfered with visibility, but they thought they saw hills on the horizon.

The women caught the passing mood of celebration and wanted to make it last longer if they could. So they brought out the last of the leavened bread, opened a jar of raspberry jam, sliced off some thick chunks of cheese, and called everyone to the table. The depressing grayness and the incessant pounding of rain dampened the festive spirit. And the rolling and tossing motions made them uncomfortable. Some family members found the food stuck in their mouths.

After that, they couldn't eat for days. Some observed that it was better to lie in the center of the barge-like boat, where there was less motion, but others thought that every place was just as bad as every other. One by one the sick ones crawled out of their hammocks and cautiously nibbled on salted crackers, and in time they began enjoying meals again, proud of themselves for adjusting to seafaring life.

Marks on the bulkhead by which they were keeping track of the forty days provided a center of interest. "Did you mark today?" "No, I didn't. I thought you wanted to." Everyone counted and recounted so often that there was no danger of missing a day, or of marking twice in one day. It was almost a ritual. While one person carefully cut the mark near the end of each day, several others watched.

Some of the animals began to need care, mostly the domestic ones that they knew well and had names for. They milked them, fed them and carried rain water to them from their full reservoir. But most of the animals continued in their torpor, which worried

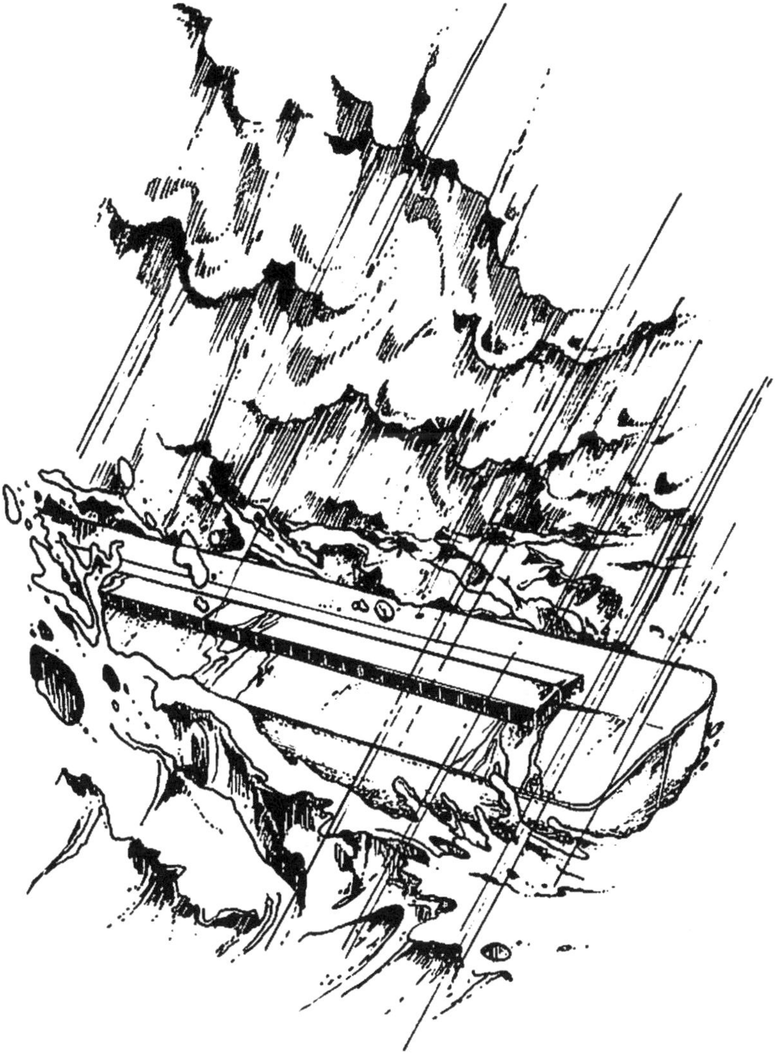

the family at first, but whenever they investigated, they found heartbeats and warm bodies. Shem and Japheth began speaking of their condition as hibernation. It was new and surprising to them, but they were glad for it, because without it they might not have managed to feed all the animals.

Noah led a family meeting each day, in which they read from the history and prophecies and talked about what God was doing. They tried singing some psalms of praise. A couple of the ladies had good voices, and raised them boldly to lead the way, and after a few days of practice, the song time became satisfying for everyone. They joked about forming a family choir and taking it on tour. Noah realized that this time together each day was important for keeping up their spirits and for helping them to get along with each other through the rest of the day.

One day in the family meeting, Noah announced that he had learned something new from studying the old prophecies. He said it was now clear to him what happened to the rebel angels, those who had left the spirit world and entered the human world. God had condemned them to die like men. So they must have perished in this cataclysm of water just like the people.

Where were they now? Noah said they were chained in darkness under the sea and would remain there until judgment day.

At that time the sea would give up its dead, they would face judgment and suffer eternal fire.

All eight family members silently began to digest this information. Here they were floating on the water, while somewhere under the sea were those terrible prisoners. Some thought, "It serves them right." Others soberly pondered how dreadful it would be to have no chance of salvation. Across Ham's mind flashed pictures of the mighty men of renown. He remembered their strange power and mysterious charm.

Quietly the family talked about demons, the old world, and the new one they were going to start. Maybe the new world would be free of demons. They certainly hoped so.

Day 40 arrived and everyone attended the marking ceremony that evening. No one doubted that the rain would stop on schedule. It had been letting up the last few days, and as darkness overtook the grayness of day, they listened and thought surely the rain had stopped already.

Falling asleep that night was not easy. So accustomed had they become to the pounding noise of rain, that this new silence kept them awake until a late hour. In the morning, sunlight streamed through the window. The women danced, the men wrestled, and everyone acted like a little child again. With much happy jostling, they managed to get through their morning chores and put a breakfast on the table. All day, whether they were washing, or studying, or playing with pet monkeys, they located themselves in the brightest sunlight possible. The mood inside the boat had never been so cheerful.

On this day and for many days after, Shem and Japheth observed the sky and the water. Though they could not see directly above because of the overhanging roof, they could see out the window. Water stretched from horizon to horizon, with no land in sight. The sun seemed to shine more harshly than it used to, and the sky was a cold blue, when it wasn't gray and drizzly.

Ham was more interested in the boat itself. How much draft did it have? He found that the water line was about halfway up the hull, so more than twenty feet of boat was submerged. Would it scrape on land, he wondered. On a hilltop, perhaps? As weeks passed by and the boat still floated, he realized the water must be at least twenty feet above the highest hills.

In the days that followed, everyone thought about the future more than the past. They took new interest in their diary notations. What was going on outside? When would they get out of the boat? What kind of houses could they make when they did get out? This new happier mood made time pass rapidly, and answers weren't long in coming.

11. The Calendar Puzzle

The red-letter fortieth day was long past. Drizzly days and sunny days had followed, more of the former than the latter, and when the men tried to measure water depth, they could only conclude that it grew deeper even after that fortieth day.

A wind came up, stronger than they had ever known in the old world. "It will blow the water away," they joked with one another. But more seriously they tried to figure out why air would move like that. The temperature was colder than they were used to, so they put on extra coats and hovered around the cooking fire more often. It seemed to them that air movement brought changes in temperature. The new look of the sun and sky began to seem almost normal. They supposed they could live with that and all the other changes. Busy days followed as the family studied nature, cared for the non-hibernating animals and performed their other chores.

One day they were startled by a sudden bump. A little rocking and settling followed, and then stillness. The huge barge, their home of five months, was no longer floating. It took awhile getting used to the feel of motionless solid ground. But ground it was; they were sure of that.

The first ones to climb up to window level reported that on one side they could see water, as before, but on the other side was a frightening wall of land. It stood almost straight up, like a hill, they declared, but steeper and higher. When the boat did not float again in the next couple of days, they recorded day 150 as the time the boat came to rest. It was exactly five months since they had entered the boat.

About two and a half months later they began seeing tops of other high hills. Someone recorded this event in the log as the first day of the tenth month of their calendar, but just after that a confusion arose about the date. Improved weather allowed them to observe that the moon was not at new. Accordingly, the month must be about four days old instead of just beginning.

This news startled everybody. Hadn't they been exceedingly careful with their record keeping? All through the stormy time they had logged and counted the thirty-day months, and now their figures were off. Ham knew he hadn't made a mistake and he blamed Shem. Shem was certain he hadn't made a mistake either. So there was quarreling for a while and more blaming.

After tempers calmed down, they considered other possibilities. Could the violence of the earth's cataclysm have affected the moon too? Did it change earth's rotation rate, perhaps speeding it up? They couldn't answer their questions, but only ask them. It would take much study of the skies to figure out what was going on.

In the meantime they continued to count days, and forty days passed. At the time of full moon, early one morning, Noah let a raven fly out the window. No one recorded the date or month of that event, because they couldn't agree on how to handle the calendar confusion. Somebody suggested that they cut the tenth month short and say that this eleventh month began with the new moon. Then they could note what day of the eleventh month Noah tested the waters with the raven. But others objected to that solution, because future readers of their history would naturally assume that months had thirty days, as they always had in the past. In the end, they simply recorded that forty days passed, and they made no reference to the calendar.

The raven did not return that day, nor the next. It never returned. With his strong wings he flew to and fro, scavenging on floating branches or carcasses and, perhaps, settling on muddy ground. So the raven became the first creature to leave the boat and live in the new world.

Noah released a dove also. This delicate bird could not find a suitable resting place, and in a short time it returned to the boat. Noah reached out his hand, the friendly little dove lit upon it, and Noah pulled her inside.

<u>After another week, the dove went out again to scout the land. This time she returned with a fresh green olive leaf</u>, and everybody knew that somewhere young seedlings were beginning to grow. A week later, Noah let the little pet out again and she never returned. The land, they knew, was now dry enough and had seeds enough for a bird to live. But was there grass enough for animals? And was it hospitable to humans? Noah talked everybody into waiting.

In the log they had only been recording days—7 days, 7days, and so forth. They did not name the months, but they knew they must be somewhere in the month of Adar, the ending of the year. But should they begin the month with the new moon they observed? Or should they begin it according to their count of days, which was four days later than the new moon? All their lives moons had lasted exactly thirty days, and according to Enoch's writings it had always been that way.

This discrepancy of four days would have been more unsettling in old world times, but the unusual water cataclysm of this past year had inured them to changes. Once they decided that they hadn't made a mistake in their records, they applied their minds to figuring out how to handle the problem.

As the new year approached, they agreed upon what to do. They would be careful with the exact date of the new year and make adjustments in their calendar at that time. So they watched the moon grow full and then begin to wane as days passed by. The new month would begin soon, too soon it seemed.

"Be sure it's the right month," Ham chided Shem, who usually was left with the job of logging their days. Japheth joined in jestingly. They might, indeed, find the beginning of a month, he said, and then discover that it wasn't Nisan after all. Underneath their lighthearted bantering, each man knew how important it was to be

accurate. Future generations would depend on their records.
The sun was moving into the sign of the Bull, and a couplet they had learned in childhood said:

> The golden Bull making his rounds
> Is first to herald each new year.

So the coming month would, indeed, be Nisan. One evening everyone was called to look into the western sky. They beheld a thin sliver of the new moon ready to follow the sun over the horizon, and beside it the Twin stars, Castor and Pollux. These stars, they knew, accompanied the first new moon of the year. It was now five days early, instead of four, but they cut the old year short and declared this day to be the start of the new year.

Noah fell in with the mood of celebration. "We will remove part of the roof," he said. The next morning the happy crew began to dismantle the roof. Years before, they had worked together carefully building and weatherproofing this roof. It had served them well. Now they were unbuilding it.

After they removed a large enough piece, all the workers climbed out onto the rooftop and had their first good look at the new world. For a time they stood shocked and speechless. They had expected some mud, but none of their imaginings had adequately prepared them for this forbidding landscape. Brown began on the mountainside around them and stretched far off into the horizon. It was punctuated with rivers and pools of water. Lush, green forests and fertile fields existed only in their memories. The cool air and gray-blue sky added to the cheerlessness of this new world. Would they ever again see the world bathed in a warm pink glow?

Japheth remembered the vanished civilization and despairingly tried to envision rebuilding. Shem saw how utterly swept away was the wickedness. Ham imagined the old cities, and a bitter question flashed through his mind: Why did God—why did his father—bring them now to this muddy brown world? They all knew they should be thankful that God chose to spare them. When they observed carefully, they noticed a few green sprouts bravely promising a future. Competing thoughts tumbled over each other in the men's minds.

When Noah finally spoke, he encouraged his sons. It was going to dry up, he said. It was going to become green. They descended into the boat again and had to tell the women that they could not move out yet.

During the next two months Noah often stood atop the roof, studying the mountain, the sky and the landscape below. This was the new world his grandchildren were going to inherit. Will they believe him if he someday describes the old world to them? If his grandchildren stand outside in depressing nighttime darkness, how will they understand the colorful, magenta nights of the old world when the heavens hung low? If they see only pale and tiny specks of stars, how will they envision the beauty of the heavens he used to know? And the rose glow of daytime sunlight? How will people born into this present harshness ever know that glory in their minds?

They won't understand, Noah realized regretfully. They will imagine the old world as like their own, but with maybe a bluer sky, whiter clouds and gentler mountains. That's what he did with his thoughts of the garden of Eden. From childhood he had read and heard about that paradise, but he always pictured it as simply a more perfect version of the earth he knew. He realized with a shock that he probably had little idea of what Adam's paradise was really like. Only Adam and Eve, who had seen it, knew what a paradise was lost.

Noah felt like Adam, standing between two worlds. Had Adam ever felt so alone as he? Only Noah and his family on this boat would understand the differences between the old and the new world. His descendants would not. Neither could they regain it. Noah thought he understood now why Adam had written so little about the garden, yet labored much to help men know God. That's what he should do too. What a grave responsibility was his!

The ground was drying. Patches of pale green on the plain below grew larger and greener. Animals in the boat began to stir from their long hibernation. The day came in which the family marked a full year of living in the boat, if it could be called a year with its five missing days.

Ten days later, God spoke again to Noah. "Go out of the ark, you and your wife and your sons and your sons' wives. And bring out every living thing that is with you, that they may multiply in the earth."

So this was it. Time to start up the new world. Noah was now 601 years old. He had been living in the barge for 365 days. Other momentous events of his life paraded through his mind, and perhaps the greatest event of them all would begin tomorrow.

12. Starting Up the New World

The family all began to work the plan they had formed during the preceding weeks. First they opened the door and made of it a ramp for disembarking. They fed the wild animals and let them go free. Bears began padding over rocks, finding their way down the mountainside. Snakes slithered quickly out of sight and the ladies were glad of that. Birds flew about, testing the air and their wings. A bearded goat stood high on a cliff silhouetted against the sky, looking at all the world as if he were king of the mountain. Deer with slender legs gracefully picked their way down a rocky slope. Cats and wolves bounded downward so silently and quickly that the people could scarcely see where their feet landed. A few smaller animals were hesitant, and the men decided to carry them until they found a more friendly environment for them.

<u>Some of the family herded domestic animals carefully so as not to lose them.</u> Others arranged loads onto pack animals, taking everything essential for planting and starting anew, and leaving items they had decided they could return for. When no one could think of one more item to run back inside for, the people, too, were ready to leave.

Ham appeared on their left from behind a crest where he had been exploring. "Come this way," he said. They needed no urging, since the gorge below them offered only a forbidding route. They made their way toward Ham and around to the west side of the mountain. There they beheld a gentler slope and, pleased with Ham's foresight, they began descending.

Starting Up the New World

Strong wind came up during the day, far stronger than had blown in the old world. They wished they could hurry down and make a shelter, but herding the animals was a cumbersome chore, and the mountain now seemed much larger than they had thought.

Land and sky stretched to meet at a distant horizon. Standing on the giant mountain, looking at the vast landscape, the people were acutely aware of how small a group of humans they were. No city down there was waiting to rent rooms to them. No orchards and fields indicated a comfortable estate where they might buy supplies. As these thoughts crossed their minds, they quickly berated themselves. "Why do I only think of good things from the old world?" several asked themselves. They should be glad, they reflected, that no criminals or crazed worshipers of false gods would be marauding and molesting them. They wouldn't have to lock their gates.

They tried to ease tension by joking about this new world of theirs. "See that vineyard down there? It's mine, and you're all invited to stop in and stay awhile."

The pack animals were great help, and by late afternoon they reached a lovely meadow with a stream flowing through. The sun shone brightly. Bushes and seedling trees gave promise of shade to come. A couple of birds greeted them with song. They loosed animals to graze. "This looks like a good place to settle," said Noah's wife. Some protested that they weren't even off the mountain yet, that they should continue to flatterland. But the sun was low in the west and they set up tents.

The next day was the Sabbath. Noah and his sons built an altar of stones and muddy earth that they found along the creek. Then they killed one of each kind of their animals and domestic fowls, to offer as burnt offerings upon the altar. During these preparations, the sky darkened with clouds and it began to rain. With some fear, they prepared the carcasses just as faithful men had done ever since Adam, and they burned them upon the altar as offerings to God.

Smoke of the offering rose up to the sky. Then God spoke to Noah and his sons. He blessed them and told them to multiply and fill the earth. Nature would be different now, God said. Wild animals would live in terror of men, and men should now eat of animals and fowl and fish, as well as of plants. But they were not to eat blood, God said. The life of the flesh is in the blood. They knew that people in the old world had eaten meat, but Noah never allowed it in his house. Now God was changing the rules. Would they like the flesh of animals? Most, especially the women, thought they wouldn't.

Governing of human life was also to be different in the new world. God reminded them that man is made in His image. Thus no one should murder another human. If someone sheds another person's blood, his own blood should be shed, and it was mankind's responsibility to see to that.

God promised that He would never again destroy the whole earth with a flood. Though man's heart is only evil continually, God would show mercy and not bring another flood. All creation would be governed by regular and predictable laws. Planting was not to be at any or all times, as in the old world, but a special season would be right for seeding, and another for harvesting.

> While the earth remains,
> Seedtime and harvest,
> And cold and heat,
> And summer and winter,
> And day and night
> Shall not cease.

"I will establish my covenant with you," said God. "I do set my bow in the cloud, and it shall be for a token of a covenant between me and the earth."

Clouds had broken in the west and sunlight began shining through. All eight people watched in awe as an ethereal bow of colors reached up from the earth, arched across the sky, and touched the earth again with its other end. They stood transfixed and speechless until at last the bow faded silently away. Never in the old world had they seen anything like that.

Faint wisps of smoke from the altar floated upward, the sun set, and stars lighted the sky as rapidly as clouds cleared the way for them. The weary people turned and walked toward their tents.

Only Shem remained. He sat upon a large rock and watched the stars. Noah looked back, and, seeing him there, went to sit beside him.

"I'm reading the sky," said Shem.

Noah looked toward the southern horizon with Shem, and together they examined the constellations that had been hidden from view during their last few months resting on the north side of the mountain peak. The Ship could be seen just about to finish its journey for the night and set in the west.

"That's us," said Shem. "We have been in the Ship and carried safely over the waters of judgment. The old prophets could have been referring to us."

Noah wasn't so sure.

"Well, it's not the final judgment," Shem agreed. "But our experience at least makes a good analogy for the safety that the ransomed of all generations will find in the Ark God provides." Shem thought it was remarkable the way their story had been in the skies since the days of Adam and Enoch. He almost laughed as he indicated the serpent stretched across most of the southern sky. "That Old Serpent can't sink the Ship. It's still struggling there in the watery deep."

Noah and Shem sat for a long time reciting to each other from Enoch's writings. On the left, was the Animal being slain for sacrifice, and the two-natured being—the Despised One—drawn as a man-horse, who was slaying it. They noted how the long Serpent was not killing even the little Animal. The Redeemer, they knew, would lay down His own life. In contrast to the Despised One, was

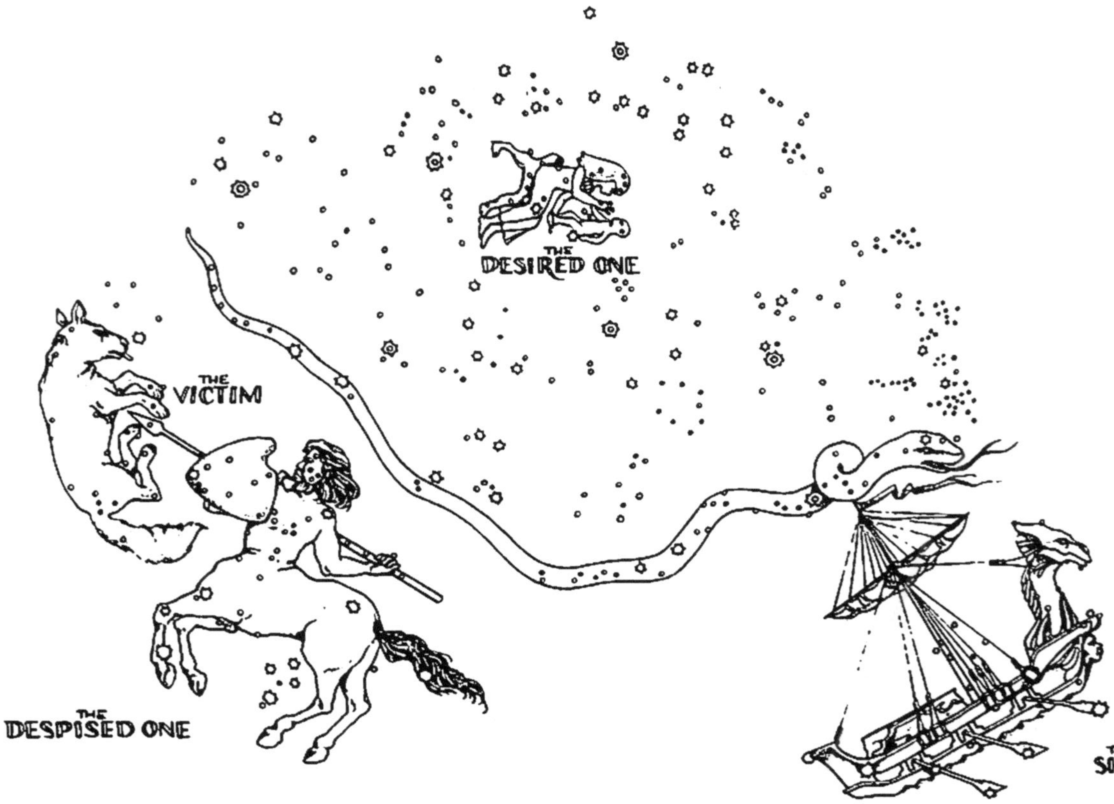
THE DESIRED ONE
THE VICTIM
THE DESPISED ONE
THE SHIP

the Desired One—a virgin and her child. "I think that is where His star will appear," said Shem. Noah nodded agreement.

During a long silence, they both thought about the history of the world. Here they sat, somewhere in the middle between Adam and the Redeemer with His final judgment.

Shem remarked, at last, that they should write the story of today. They should remember God's words and record them for their children. Noah agreed. They repeated to each other all the words of God and set them in memory so they could write them accurately when daylight came.

Not weary in the least, they rose to walk toward their tents. And even the rumbling they now heard within the mountain did not dampen their hope for the future.

13. Trouble at Ararat

Some years later, the landscape was considerably improved at the foot of the mountain on its north side. Vineyards, orchards, grain fields, and animal herds were thriving. The human family had grown, too. The early years of resettlement had gone almost as planned. Everyone helped to plant the first fields, and as soon as there were enough animals and supplies to start a second farm, one of Noah's sons chose a new location and everyone helped him get started. This procedure was repeated until the three sons and later some grandsons all had flourishing estates.

The mountain which they called Ararat sometimes smoked and sometimes spewed lava. The earth now and then rumbled fearsomely. But the seasons came and went with regularity just as God had promised.

During the first few years Noah was cheered by the happy voices of little grandchildren. These children knew nothing of the terrible sins of the old world, he contemplated. They were a fresh start and a hope for the future.

Almost before he knew it, those children were grown and having families of their own. And then again, so that in some families Noah could count five generations including himself, and the new world was not yet a hundred years old.

For a time everyone worried about a couple of children who looked pale and sickly, but those grew to be just as robust as the others. Noah had known people as white as that in the old world. Some children had hair blacker than night. One of the shepherds observed that close interbreeding in the animals was causing variations to appear in the animal kinds. Perhaps the same thing was happening with humans, he said.

Some families moved out from the shadow of the mountain and set up a town they called Aratta. People were starting to fill the world as God had commanded. Exploring groups traveled far. Westward they found a large deep sea they called the Black Sea. They mapped its shores and sometimes ventured along the rivers which flowed into it.

One group returned from the far north and reported severe cold and ice which had stopped them. In subsequent trips they confirmed that ice was advancing southward. That brought fear into many hearts. Maybe ice will cover the earth, they worried. It would bring the end of the world. But Noah reminded them of God's promise that seedtime and harvest, and cold and heat, and summer and winter would continue until God's plan for this earth was finished.

Other explorers went southward and found two rivers flowing through a sunny, fertile valley. They returned with wondrous descriptions of that land and decided to name the rivers Tigris and Euphrates after two of the rivers in Eden, which they had heard about from the tales of their fathers. The younger generation was always puzzled about those tales, because they told of the Eden River parting and becoming four, while they could plainly see that the reverse happened; rivers flow together and become one.

Shem helped the geographers by giving them astronomy lessons. From the stars he could plot their latitude on the globe of the earth. With the help of their time-keeping instruments, they also plotted longitude, and Shem noted that the land mass they were now settled on had been under the ocean in the old world. Farmers could use Shem's astronomy lessons, too. By this time he had concluded from the sky that there were more days per year, as though the earth had speeded its rotation. Twelve 30-day months did not equal a year anymore, as the books said, and they had to arrange a new calendar.

All Shem's children and grandchildren and nieces and nephews who wanted to learn came to Shem's school. From the sky they learned to read times and seasons of the earth—when to welcome a new year, when to plant, when to harvest. And that was only a beginning of sky knowledge. The times of God's plan for the earth could be learned too, by the diligent.

Letters of the alphabet were placed in the twelve signs that marked the sun's path through the stars. Thus every letter was surrounded with meaning, and children could remember them easily. For instance, the letter *beth*, or *b*, was associated with the Bowman, or Archer. Students learned that this half-horse and half-man sign in the sky stood for a man of two natures, the mighty King of the earth who will come forth to conquer. The beth symbol was also the numeral 2. Instead of a sky alphabet, children could learn a tree alphabet, in which beth was associated with the birch tree, which put out its new leaves early in the spring.

Each letter and word and number was rich with meaning. Everything fit together in beautiful patterns. Reality was close and exciting when one was listening to Shem. And all knowledge revealed more about the great Creator God.

During those early decades of the new world, Noah often pondered the problem of how man should govern himself. The words of God that he and Shem had recorded said, "Whoso sheddeth man's blood, by man shall his blood be shed." It was man's responsibility to comply with that. So far no Cain had murdered anybody but there were lesser quarrels about who owned certain wandering donkeys and oxen, where boundary lines were, and what a man should give to the new home when his daughter marries. Stealing was sometimes suspected and murder would someday happen.

To his sorrow, Noah could discern a rebellious spirit that had begun in his son Ham and had grown menacingly in Canaan and Cush and other of Ham's sons. Sin had not disappeared in the Great Flood. Yes, people would need laws and fair ways to judge a murderer and other transgressors, and to carry out the unpleasant task of shedding the blood of a murderer. Each time Noah arbitrated a dispute, he wrote down the case as an example for future cases like it. Some of his descendants were glad that Noah kept law and order and they learned from him how they should manage it in settlements of their own. But some resented Noah.

Shem stayed close to Noah and helped him. Noah was over 600 years old and his sons over 100, and beside them, all the world seemed made up of striplings under about 50 years of age. Far too many of the younger generations did not want to know God. Often Noah felt lonely and discouraged. Was this new world going to turn out as bad as the old?

On one of his most discouraging days, Noah drank too much of the wine from his plentiful vineyard, so much that he lost control of his senses. Alone in his tent, he couldn't reach for another cup. Feeling flushed and overheated, he lay down, tossed his cloak aside, and fell into a drunken sleep.

A few moments later, Ham came by unexpectedly and stepped into the tent to see his father. He was shocked at first to see Noah in such a condition, but his shock turned to a perverse delight in the scene. There lay the man who had ruled Ham's life with strong authority for many years, the man who preached about God and righteousness, the man who was teaching others how to govern themselves. There he lay, drunk and naked. "I must tell my brothers," Ham thought, and he ran to get Shem and Japheth.

The brothers, upon hearing Ham's story, took no delight in it. They did not want to see their father in that drunken state, and they knew he would be ashamed when he woke up. "You go cover him," said one. "No, you cover him," said the other.

They agreed upon a plan where both would share the task. They took a cloak and carried it between them. Holding it high, they backed into the tent carefully and slowly until they reached

Noah's couch. With faces still turned away, they laid the cloak upon him and never once glimpsed his nakedness.

When Noah woke up and saw that he was covered with a different cloak, he asked questions until he learned what had transpired while he was drunk. Noah was ashamed of his own actions that day, but was saddened even more by Ham's actions. With his deep insight into human nature, he understood that Ham's behavior was not a one-time lapse of good manners. It came, instead, from a rebellious heart that he had seen growing quite alarmingly in Ham and in his sons.

The whole community was gossiping now. Some enjoyed the juicy story and were glad that Noah had been caught in his drunkenness. "Serves him right," they said to each other. Some didn't say that out loud, but in their private thoughts they, too, were glad that Noah had been disgraced.

Others truly loved the old patriarch Noah and the God he represented to them. "Don't talk about it," they urged, to no avail. Some took sides against Ham. He should have remained quiet, they judged, and not stirred up dissension.

But what was done could not be undone. Relations among the families grew more strained until it seemed the best solution was for some of them to move away and begin new settlements elsewhere. As preparations moved forward, it was not only the dissatisfied ones who planned to resettle, but others, too, were lured by explorers' reports or by wanting to obey God and spread throughout the earth.

Before the first group left, Noah called together the heads of families to listen to his patriarchal prophecies and his last words to those departing. First, he reminded everyone of the things he and Shem and other fathers had taught of God, creation, sin, redemption, the Great Flood, and other important matters and urged them to pass these teachings on to their children in all generations.

Then Noah came to the sensitive matter of blessings and cursing, of the future that he could see for each of his sons. He began with the youngest, to get the dreadful words over with quickly, but he could not bring himself to pronounce the name Ham. His own dear son had been through so much with him. Together they had built the ark and had come over the waters from the old world to the new. In the construction and other handiwork, Ham had been more help than anyone. Yet Noah must tell the curse upon his progeny. Instead of the name Ham, Noah pronounced the name of Ham's youngest son Canaan, saying, "Cursed be Canaan; a servant of servants shall he be unto his brethren."

Noah turned toward his middle son Shem. He knew that Shem was the son through whom God would bring the promised Seed. All mankind would enjoy boundless spiritual blessing when that Seed came. Noah said, "Blessed be the Lord God of Shem; and Canaan shall be his servant."

Then Noah turned to his eldest son. Japheth had joined his brother Shem in covering Noah on that fateful day, and Noah understood that as the two brothers had entered his tent together, so would their descendants enter a tent together, the tent of spiritual blessings from the true God. Noah prophesied, "God shall enlarge Japheth and he shall dwell in the tents of Shem; and Canaan shall be his servant."

Family members listened to these blessings and the cursing from Noah. Shem's God, they heard, was Jehovah. Japheth's family would enlarge their minds and hearts, and worship that God too. And Canaan, or Ham's descendants, would serve them both.

Those were heavy thoughts. Coming from wise old Noah as they did, they made people think about the future for a few days. What kind of world were they going to make? But most people soon stopped thinking about future generations because their own lives were busy, and daily work swallowed up those thoughts.

Ham's oldest son Cush did not forget. "What did I do to deserve a curse like that?" he asked bitterly. He nursed his already rebellious spirit, little knowing what a terrible power lay therein.

14. Land of the Two Rivers

Reports came back from the new settlements. Those who had gone to the plain where flowed the Tigris and Euphrates rivers extolled the richness of that land. It grew date palms and lush fields of barley and wheat. There was no lack of pasturage for cows and sheep and goats nor of food to feed the pigs. People could build reed houses or mud brick houses, depending on where they located.

Some traders from the plain returned to the Caucasus Mountains north of Ararat to get copper and obsidian which they used at first for necessary tools and, later, for decorations. Other men built boats and explored for metals and precious stones around the gulf into which the rivers flowed. Some tribes had a knowledge of metallurgy passed down from their fathers. They were told that the knowledge and skills began in the old world and had come through the Great Flood particularly in the person of Ham, who was the survivor most talented in those arts.

A convenient source of metal would help people living on the plain. Farmers there had good clay from which they made temporary sickles. When baked well, these sickles were hard and could be made sharp enough to do considerable work before they broke. But metal, when it was imported, was far better.

At first people also made bowls from the clay. But then someone discovered a technique for making stoneware. The lowlands had abundant supplies of lime and of natron, which was found in certain salt-water lakes. These ingredients when mixed with water formed a caustic soda that, in turn, was mixed into crushed blue minerals. The soda ate into the minerals, consuming them, and made a messy but high quality cement. Then river silt was kneaded into the cement and stonemakers formed bowls or pots or whatever they wanted from it. They turned their vessels on a potter's wheel or sometimes used molds. After the vessels dried they looked like polished stone and were every bit as strong.

Besides the artistic Hamite families, many Shemites came to live on the plain, so many, in fact, that the plain came to be called Shemer, or Sumer. Numerous Shemite herdsmen were scattered in the river valleys. Some groups of Shemites settled in towns, and an important early town of theirs was Akkad, which they built at the mouth of the Euphrates River.

Sometime later, a tribe of Japhethites descended into the plain, just as if they remembered the words of Noah saying that they would dwell in the tents of Shem. This particular tribe had blacker hair than other people they knew, so they called themselves the "black heads." These black heads liked town life better than nomadic life, and they proceeded to build towns of their own. One of their first was called Eridu after the name of a famous old-world city.

Though Eridu was only a little cluster of modest buildings at first, its settlers called it a city anyway. And they told their children that Eridu was the oldest city in the world. It was made right after the lands and sea were created, they said, and it had kings before the Flood and after the Flood.

Eridu was located near the mouth of the Euphrates River, but it was far south of Akkad because the gulf waters had receded quite alot since Akkad was settled, making the river longer than before. A town called Erech also grew up nearby.

The black-headed people had excellent artistic skills. They made wall panels and other decorations for their buildings from copper, as well as from local limestone, shale and seashells. When beautiful lapis lazuli was imported, along with gold and silver, they incorporated these elegant materials into their art.

Land of the Two Rivers

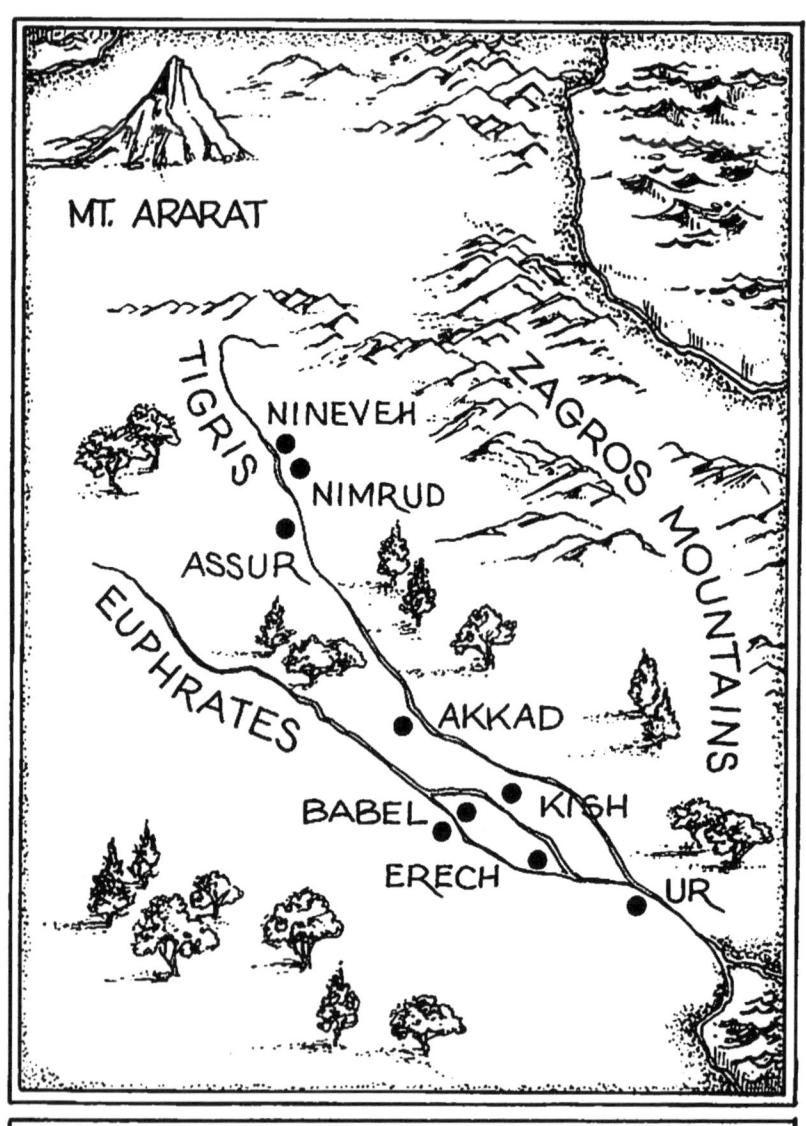

People were creating comfortable lives for themselves and beginning to spread over the earth as Noah had taught. They overcame most problems that faced them, but many feared the wild animals. Boars looked threatening, and field workers ran for cover when one of them appeared. Dragons never stopped growing, and occasionally one reached monstrous size and terrorized a whole town. Even little jackals came in pairs by night and snatched lambs from the flocks. Wild beasts seemed to be multiplying faster than men. Only the dragons were decreasing in numbers, as there was never enough food to satisfy their giant appetites. Their scarcity made a dragon all the more frightening when he did appear. He was like a legendary monster from the old world.

Cush dwelt beside the Euphrates and, as his descendents multiplied there, the community came to be called Kish, a form of Cush's name. This son of Ham, this Hermes, retained a resentful and bitter heart. He determined that his family would not serve the other families, as Noah had prophesied. They would become powerful; they would rule; they would defy God.

He thought obsessively upon Ham's stories of mighty men of the times before the Great Flood. Those god-men were powerful, and Cush coveted that power. He resolved to find again the shadowy secrets of the spirit world that men used to know, and one night in a dark room he saw what he was waiting for. A robed figure looking like a man, but not a man, appeared to him.

Cush returned often to his seances, and contacted the spirit again and again. He told the spirit's messages to others who were interested, and he became known as a prophet. What was to be the future of the world? Cush gave answers. What did the gods want worshipers to do? Cush gave answers. Who was king of heaven? When would the promised Seed appear? The words of Cush's prophecies were usually confusing, and people listened with fear.

Cush chose certain men to be priests, and they were busy most of the time with seances and sacrifices and other religious activity.

They busied themselves little with the repair of irrigation canals and other government functions. People paid tax money to Cush, and that money was used for both the religion and the government.

Many citizens wanted to worship God, so the leaders didn't let them know everything that went on in the temple. Much of it was secret. Cush's inner circle of trusted priests joined in his seances and sometimes they saw a globe of light or a human-like figure appear from nowhere and attest to the messages a spirit gave.

The priests devised ways to imitate these spirits. By trickery, they made a form or a light appear and then a voice speak. In this manner they led many worshipers into thinking they heard messages from God. Thus, with real spirits and pretend spirits, Cush's religious system kept growing.

Cush tried to do what the spirits told him to do, but that was not easy. Each spirit wanted to be worshiped as a god. Some of them demanded sacrifices and other rituals. Each god claimed a constellation or a star as his own, so that star stories as the priests taught them were different from what Noah and Shem had taught in the beginning of the new world. In time, the stories became so completely twisted that the Serpent was no longer the evil one who would be crushed in the end. Instead, he was the god to worship, the highest power in the air.

It all became so complicated that Cush and his priests set up a school to train young men for the priesthood. Students helped with the work of preparing for sacrifices and other rites that worshipers participated in. They learned about the many gods, and those who showed themselves ready were initiated into secrets of black magic and divining and other powers that came from the demon gods.

Only the very highest priests knew that at the center of this temple system was the worship of the creature who had appeared to Eve in the garden of Eden. That serpent, they were taught, had brought knowledge to all mankind. Thus he was the light of the heavens, the Sun, and all should worship him. This powerful god had an army of angels who helped him rule the world. Those angels, too, were called gods.

It was not long before the temple system needed young women, as well as men, so a school was set up for them, too. Some worked as maids, cleaning and cooking and keeping the place running smoothly. Others became priestesses who were taught that they would have the high honor of marrying gods. Each priestess, at various times, was to enter a darkened room where she might see a vision of her god-husband. Or if the god didn't come, a human might substitute. That would be the earthly symbol of her marriage to the god, but the god was waiting for her in the after life.

Boys in the school also learned how to manage business affairs. People usually paid their taxes in animals, grain, beer, and other products, so there were many accounts to keep for the temple, palace and other government projects.

Cush's plans were turning out well for him so far, but he had bigger plans yet. The spirit promised him more power if he would lead all men to rebel against God. Thus when a son was born to Cush, he named the child Nimrod. He taught Nimrod when he was very young why he was named, "Let us rebel." They were rebelling against God, he said. He told the child that he would someday be ruler over all people and that the world would bow at his feet. He placed high hopes in this son.

Nimrod grew up believing his father and the spirits. He was destined to be the ruler of the world, and this made him strong and fearless. While he was yet a youth, Nimrod learned to hunt. Once he killed a bull with his bare hands. Then in the power of the bull, it was said, he turned around and killed a lion with his bare hands. Word spread far and wide that Nimrod was as strong as a bull, and artists drew pictures showing him wearing the horns of a bull.

Nimrod became a skilled archer, and he trained other young men in the toils and dangers of the chase. He was hailed as a hero, and towns threatened by wild beasts more than once called upon him and his companions for help.

Nimrod tamed some leopards. These spotted cats were the fastest animals he knew, and Cush helped him breed them and train them for hunting. With leopards, Nimrod could capture even the swift jackals. Nimrod and his father also bred and trained dogs for hunting. Everybody said, "Nimrod is a mighty hunter before the Lord."

Cush and Nimrod decided to set up a new and better city, to be named for Nimrod, and to be located across the river from Kish. Tax money would pay for a luxurious palace, a school and all the religious and government buildings they wanted. Nimrod was king of the city, and he oversaw its planning and construction. Brick-makers, builders, merchants and others began moving into the city of the popular hero Nimrod.

Nimrod was not a handsome man, but with his wealth and power and fame he could win any woman he wanted for his wife. He chose the beautiful Semiramis, who, though suddenly raised to the high position of queen, quickly learned to live as she thought a queen ought to live. She had servants and elegant clothes, more than she needed. She basked in the honor of being the king's wife, while at the same time encouraging other admirers and being unfaithful to Nimrod.

Nimrod and Semiramis planned feasts and celebrations to honor the gods and to keep the people of their city happy. The most joyful celebration of all was held at the beginning of each new year. Music and strong drink and banqueting put the people in a holiday mood, and then Nimrod and his mighty men, with chariots and musicians and fleet leopards, paraded through the streets. People followed, especially women. They raised their hands and cried after their hero Nimrod.

> The mighty Nimrod goes forth,
> The city kneels before him.
> Beside strong Nimrod the Bull,
> While his servants play the flute,
> Goes all the city, exultant!

Watching such a parade, Cush knew it was time for his next move.

15. The Tower of Bel

The mighty Nimrod, with his strong young men, were now invincible. His hunters turned into warriors, and nowhere in all the settlements of the plain was there such an array of power. They could go anywhere and set up a governor of their choice and no one could oppose them. With Cush urging him on, Nimrod went first to Erech and Akkad and easily brought those cities under his rule. Soon all the cities of the plain were his. And that meant all the cities of the world were his.

Up north where the Tigris flowed fresh from the hills, lived people not yet a part of Nimrod's kingdom, and something had to be done about that. On the plain, if Nimrod ruled a city he also ruled the herdsmen and farmers in its surrounding area. So what the north needed was cities. He went up there and built a new city called Nimrud and some others nearby, so near that in time they all came to be called by the name of the largest in the cluster, Nineveh.

Everywhere that Nimrod conquered, he collected workers and taxes to strengthen his empire. Cush's young priests who were trained in the temple schools spread to all the cities and set up their kind of worship throughout the land. Cush was gaining power and was almost ready for his final, bold move.

But one circumstance in the kingdom constantly angered him. That was the activity of Shem's preachers. Too many people listened to those preachers. As long as they were alive and undermining his religious system, Cush could not rest.

One day he said to Nimrod, "I have an oracle from the gods,

The Tower of Bel

from the most high god. If you do his bidding and get rid of Shem's preachers, your kingdom will live forever."

It took no persuading. Nimrod declared war on the preachers. He determined to kill every last one of them. "Let my kingdom live forever," he said. His warriors paraded through the streets of the capital to display their strength. Then they fanned out to the cities to find and kill those vexing preachers. They would get them—those men who were unarmed and untrained in the arts of war, those men whose only power lay in the words they spoke.

All over the kingdom some citizens reported the whereabouts of preachers, and others helped them to hide or escape. The war was not over quickly. Soldiers and guards on the rounds of their other duties were continually on the lookout for another victim of the hunt.

In the capital city new plans were taking shape. Now that there was a northern city named after Nimrod, and there were few preachers or citizens with power to object, Nimrod announced with public celebrations the renaming of the capital. It would be called Bel in honor of the most high god, the god of the sun and of fire. The inner circle of priests knew, while most people did not, that behind the name Bel was the Serpent himself, the one who was giving power to Nimrod.

To make the city worthy of the god and of the world system over which it ruled, it would be enlarged. Fine buildings would be added. A wall with fortifications and towers would encompass the whole. The wall, when finished, would measure 360 stadia to symbolize the full circle of the earth, for this city was to be the capital of the world. Forever.

Queen Semiramis took special pleasure in the wall and thought of it as her own project. Construction began and, as each new stadia stretched out, she saw her realm growing larger. "All within this wall is mine," she gloated. "I am Queen of this domain."

The crowning attraction of the new city would be the Tower of Bel. It would be the highest structure ever built in this new world, and at its top would be a shrine to Bel himself and his sky gods, a shrine to the stars.

"Let us make a name for ourselves," Cush said to Nimrod and the priests.

The King and the power-hungry priests echoed his words. "Yes, let us make a name for ourselves."

Cush's best architects were summoned, and they designed a marvelous structure consisting of a series of terraced platforms one atop the other, each smaller than the one below it, and all together reaching an unparalleled height. At the very top they placed the shrine.

So that the massive structure would not be plain or monotonous to the eye, they built into their plan the best artistic devices they knew. The outer walls of each terrace would have recessed and protruding panels so the sunlight could play there and cast interesting shadows. Corner panels were narrower than the others, which helped them to look like strong pillars holding up the tower. The walls of each platform sloped inward gently as they rose, and this, too, gave an appearance of strength. And only the architects knew that the walls must curve ever so slightly or else the structure would appear weak to a person looking across the length of a wall.

Many other professional secrets the architects brought to their task, knowledge of mathematics and construction that Cush had learned from Ham, and Ham had learned in the old world. The young architects were proud to plan a building like legendary ones they had heard of but had never seen.

Soon Nimrod's builders were ready to start. From every town they gathered workers and money. They baked thousands and thousands of bricks. They brought natural bitumen from pits located on the plain. They built up the solid inner core at the same time as they built the wall around it. Outer walls were thick with many layers of brick and were carefully made to be thicker at the bottom of each terrace than at the top. Bricks were set with bitumen, and

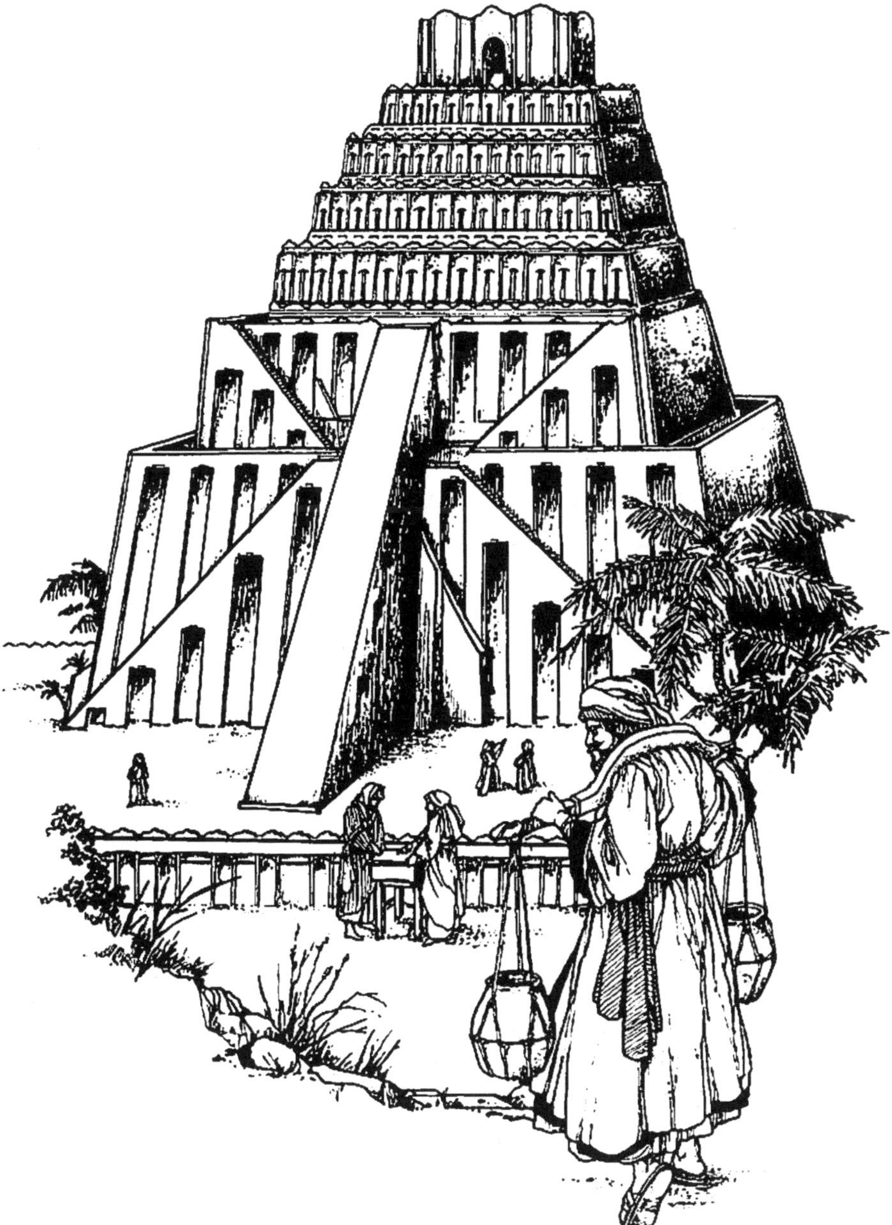

reeds inlaid within the structure helped to bind it together. Each terrace was painted a different color, and decorations of carved or cast limestone panels and inlaid shell added elegance.

After much labor, the magnificent tower was finished. Though the city walls and other projects were still incomplete, the King sent word throughout his kingdom that all men should come to the capital city for a celebration at the tower.

Cush and Nimrod were sitting on top of their world. They had killed most of the preachers and soon all people would come to their tower and worship Bel.

The city was astir with preparations, and roads were alive with travelers. It looked as if everything would happen according to plan. But it was not to be.

The first disquieting sign came when travelers saw a new star in the south. Night after night it grew until it was a huge and brilliant ball as large as the moon. "The Queen of Heaven!" people exclaimed. "She is angry." They tried to hide.

The weather turned stormy and violent, and one night those near the city itself were horrified as they saw fire from heaven come down and strike the tower. Travelers turned and ran. Screaming and confusion were everywhere.

There followed a series of earthquakes. For several days the rumblings and shakings kept people in a constant state of fear. They never knew when another quake would hit. And each night the moon which was not a moon rolled menacingly along the horizon.

People were frightened by those terrors in the earth and sky, but worse yet were the terrors within them. They couldn't seem to think straight. When they tried to speak, the right words wouldn't come. They used words that almost said what they meant, because they could no longer find words which said exactly what they meant. It was as if they used to be intelligent like men but now they were simple like children.

When a traveler tried to talk with other travelers, he could not understand them. Their words and the sounds of their speaking were strange. People shouted, but it did not help. It was like being among a pack of animals rather than among fellow human beings. People felt angry and frightened by turns. To escape the confusion, most hurried to their homes and found, to their relief, that their own families could understand them.

In the capital city, confusion was worse than on the roads. The temple school was in chaos. And that was mild compared with the pandemonium at construction sites and the shouting between merchants and customers on the streets.

Priests in charge of the tower dedication quarreled at the tops of their voices. Certain priests could understand certain others, and they formed themselves into groups. Days of struggle followed in which some priests were killed and others fled to the towns of their youth.

Turbulence continued to mount. Thieves looted houses and stole animals. Nimrod's appointees could not keep order in the towns they were ruling. Some abandoned their responsibilities because they could not make their speech understood; others left because of the people's rising anger against Nimrod.

Only slowly did it dawn on people that the babble they heard around them was language that could be understood by somebody. Though a man couldn't understand what a cluster of people were saying, he could see that they understood each other. Something new was happening under the sun.

Some men made a hasty decision to move their families away from Nimrod's kingdom. The first to load up their belongings and go were those who had previously explored and knew a suitable place to relocate. Others, seeing the little caravans, decided it would be a good idea for them to move, too. In a few days the roads were busy again, with everyone traveling away from the capital this time, instead of toward it. "Babel," they called the city. "Babel, Babel!" they mocked. They hoped they would never see it again, and they wondered why they once had trusted Nimrod.

Some families could not leave so quickly because they wanted first to rescue their young daughters who were temple maidens and their sons who were in the temple school learning to be priests. Families in the capital and in every outlying town of Nimrod's kingdom were tied to his system in this way. Fathers and brothers hastened to the capital to see what they could do. In the utter confusion there, many of them managed to spirit away the young people they had come for.

Nimrod's Uncle Canaan and his many sons traveled westward to fertile, green lands they knew of beside the Great Sea. His other uncles traveled southward, and Grandfather Ham joined one of those families. Nimrod's several brothers also moved southward into various locations in Arabia.

Shemites and Japhethites who were on the plain scattered too. Nimrod's kingdom was no more.

Many a traveling family lay on their mats at night looking at the stars. Sometimes a young father pointed out the Serpent or the Dragon for his child and began to recount its story as he had learned it back home. He would begin to explain that the Serpent was more powerful than any god in the sky. Then an older voice would interrupt and say, "No, don't teach the children that. The Serpent's head will be crushed in the end. See that god up there with his foot on the Dragon's head? He's the powerful one."

Was the Serpent, and the spirit power behind him, going to win in the end? Or was he going to be fatally crushed by a stronger power? Which god should they worship? No one seemed sure anymore.

16. Aftermath

North of Ararat, where the vast mountain spread across the southern horizon hiding the awesome star, a solemn group of men sat talking. These were Shem and some of his remaining preachers. Father Noah had joined the meeting too. The presence of Shem and Noah quieted the fear which beat in the hearts of the younger men. Noah and Shem, being centuries old, inspired much veneration in the others, none of whom could claim even two centuries. A good many, in fact, were like Shem's great-great-grandson Eber, just youths in their thirties.

The youths looked to the two revered fathers for guidance in their work and for courage in these difficult times. The two fathers, after all, had lived in the old world, something they themselves could only read or hear about. And the two had witnessed and survived God's terrible judgment upon the world. Thus if the world was shaking again, the best place to be was in the presence of Noah and Shem.

The young preachers, and Shem too, were reporting to each other the turbulent events on the plain of Sumer. Some of these preachers had lived on the plain trying to fight the apostasy until they were forced to go into hiding. Others were still under the close tutelage of Shem and had made periodic trips to the towns to encourage believers and to bring to them the latest messages from Shem. Even since Nimrod had declared war, they were often able through their contacts to meet with the faithful.

For some years now the preachers had been issuing strong

warnings against the evils of Nimrod's system, and they were branded as enemies. Now they pieced together reports from all the preachers and tried to make sense of the confusing events of the past few weeks. One man commented on how appropriate it was that fire from heaven should strike the tower that was erected for the worship of fire and the heavenly bodies. Other men agreed.

Most traveling preachers could not communicate with their people on their latest trip. Some preachers could not find their people. Houses were empty or were inhabited by someone they did not know. Roads were alive with travelers moving in all directions, and few could understand them or give information. Through strange experiences they came to realize that people were speaking new kinds of languages.

It was a judgment from God, said Shem. It was God's way of stopping Nimrod's rebellion before it destroyed the whole world.

Numerous preachers were missing. They didn't know how many had been killed and how many were now speaking other tongues and were among the emigrant groups that were going to start new lives far away from Babel. May they always remain faithful to the Lord God, said the preachers in soft tones to each other as they spoke of the absent men. They expected never to see them again on this earth. Their depleted numbers graphically showed the remaining men that this was not an ordinary happy conference. In fact, they had to realize that this conference may be their last.

The rumors about Nimrod—what had really happened? One preacher reported a story he had heard that Nimrod was killed by a wild boar. A couple of others had heard the same story. After considering that and comparing it with other rumors, the men decided that most probably it was just a story started by those who wanted Nimrod to look like a hero and brave hunter right up to the end.

Many people in the plain blamed the preachers themselves for Nimrod's death. Everyone knew that Shem's men were Nimrod's most potent enemies. They knew that some people followed Shem's

Aftermath

teachings openly and many more followed secretly. It was as if golden cords coming from the mouths of preachers drew men toward them, and away from Nimrod. Nimrod's mighty men were quick to accuse the preachers of assassinating Nimrod.

The darkest rumor of all was that Semiramis was responsible for his murder. However it happened, Nimrod was dead.

A tribunal of men from some leading towns managed to get their hands on Nimrod's body and, acting according to a law that they thought came from Noah, determined its disposal. It should not have honorable burial, they declared. Nimrod's crimes had been too heinous. He was the cause of this judgment from God. Disaster had come upon all men because of this one man. They cut his body into pieces and sent a piece to each town as a warning to all.

The preachers put together this story from bits of information reported by various members of their group. Perhaps there was a fragment of justice in blaming them for what happened to Nimrod. Their teachings at least had some influence on people of the plain.

On following days the men turned their deliberations to strategy for the future. They needed to spread out in the world as Noah had taught from the beginning. They no longer would use stories in the stars as part of their preaching. Nimrod's system had so corrupted that knowledge that it would not be useful anymore in pointing men to the Creator God.

Should they go to live in towns? Just now the towns were in utter confusion. About the only cooperative action there was the severing of Nimrod's body. Men's anger could agree on that. But they fought over who should govern. Canals and buildings were abandoned half-finished. Commerce was all but halted. Society had fallen apart, and it could not readily be rebuilt.

Eber thought he would live a nomadic life with his flocks. Too much evil lodged in towns, and perhaps he could show the world a better way. Some of the other preachers were inclined to agree with him.

Eber now had a little son to think about, as his wife had just presented him with a beautiful baby boy. They determined not to raise the child in a town. A name for the child? Name him Peace, said one, and help him bring peace again to the troubled world. But Eber didn't think he was an effective leader for that. Other friends had other suggestions. Name him Division or Earthquake, said some, and in the end that is what they did. His name was Peleg in commemoration of the tumultuous events in the year of his birth. This name in the family tree would serve to remind people of the year when the earth was divided—family against family, city against city, worshiper of the evil god against worshiper of the true God, language separating from language. Everyone fervently hoped that Peleg would know a better world when he grew up.

Down on the plain, Semiramis was about the busiest person alive. Now that there was no king, would she go back to being a humble lady of the streets? By no means. She had more plots and strategy in her head than anyone else. And she had a spirit god telling her what to do. She would continue to be Queen.

Semiramis caught on more quickly than most people to what was happening with people's speech. She gathered all the priests who spoke her tongue and they worked together. The priests liked her plans because they saw a chance for their own survival. With much fighting and intrigue, they ousted other groups of priests and held on to the temples and the fire-blackened tower for themselves. With other henchmen, some of whom had been Nimrod's warriors, Semiramis held on to the palace.

Cush, in fear for his life, went into hiding.

While chaos continued in the city and increasing numbers of people deserted it, Semiramis and her top priests were already spreading the rumor which was at the center of their plan for power. The Serpent had killed Nimrod, they said, pleased with themselves for this strategy. The Serpent killed him in fulfillment of the prophecy that he would crush the heel of the Seed.

Nimrod was the Seed? People were astounded. Those in the

city who spoke the same language as Semiramis and her priests passed this word from house to house. Nimrod, the Seed? Then he would live again, said knowing voices. He would live to crush the head of the Serpent. People argued agitatedly. Everyone's temper was short in those days.

    Little by little more of the story came out. Nimrod had descended to the underworld and Semiramis was going down to rescue him. He could be freed only if enough women mourned for him. Semiramis started things by sending her female servants to the streets beside the tower to begin the weeping. Other women, seeing them, felt guilty and decided they should mourn too. Hadn't Nimrod given them a good life? Shouldn't they help him now?

    For three days the mourning continued. Semiramis gloated. She was turning people's hearts back to their hero. She would keep her power.

    On the third day the mourning turned into celebration. Nimrod had returned from the underworld, the mourners were told. They should begin feasting and dancing. Semiramis provided intoxicating drinks, and the streets rang with laughter and loud voices. It was the first merriment the city had seen since the disaster struck.

    The priests were overjoyed and planned that the lamentations for Nimrod should be repeated every year. Other religious activities were resumed, and the people were once again immersed in worship of the many gods of the sky. The moon-star retreated. Partly with hope and partly with terror, people felt they must keep the gods happy.

    Stories about Semiramis again circulated. Nimrod in his spirit form had visited Semiramis, the gossips said. She was now going to bear a child, and it would be Nimrod himself reborn as a baby, a god-child.

    No one saw much of Semiramis after that, and in time people forgot that she had been their human queen. If she was the mother of a god, then she must be a goddess herself, and in people's minds that is what she was—the Queen of Heaven, the mother of gods. In different languages she came to have other names. Artists made pictures and statues of the mother goddess holding the holy infant.

New pictures and statues of grown-up Nimrod showed his appearance as fair and handsome. He had ceased to be an ugly and powerful man. He was now a god.

17. Gods and Goddesses

No one could put the kingdom together again. Out in the hills and caves lived the most degenerate of men who had fled the towns. Elsewhere, men were wandering and fleeing. Hurricanes and floods often troubled the land of the two rivers. Rumblings in the earth kept people terrorized. The gods must be on a rampage.

In time a new priest-king arose in the town of Babel, and his many priests tried to keep their gods happy. Morning and evening the priests set two-course meals before images of the gods. They served lighter meals at other times of day. They washed the gods' hands before feeding them. They changed their clothes at regular times and dressed them in festival garments when special days arrived. The gods must be cared for just as a king is cared for.

The farmers and workers, all the ordinary people of the city, brought sacrifices and offerings to the gods—bulls, lambs, wild boars, ducks, cranes and other animals and birds; oil; loaves made from wheat and barley flour; sweets made from cream, honey and dates; and drinks of beer, wine and milk in vessels of gold and alabaster.

When worshipers entered a temple, they could glimpse its god only at a distance, as he stood on a pedestal far back in a cella. On festival days they got a better view as the image was paraded through the streets.

Stories about a god in Babel called Tammuz sometimes sounded like stories about Nimrod. Tammuz descended to the underworld, and every spring the women wept to bring him back. The goddess was now called Ishtar. She was Queen of Heaven, or

Queen of the Universe, and her stories sounded a lot like those of Semiramis. She, too, went to the underworld, and she demanded to be let in.

> If you open not the gate so that I may enter,
> I will smash the door, I will shatter the bolt,
> I will crush the doorpost, I will move the doors.

If Ishtar was not let in, she was going to raise the dead and loose them so there would be more ghosts than living people on the earth. Demons in the underworld didn't want the dead raised up, so her threat worked, according to the story.

People listened to the story with shivers of fear. Ghosts were like demons, and demons were everywhere in their lives and minds. Demons brought illness. Demons haunted houses. Demons caused crop failure. There was no escaping demons for:

> Doors and bolts do not stop them;
> High walls and thick walls they cross like waves;
> They leap from house to house;
> Under the doors they slip like serpents.

Troubled people got priest-magicians to recite incantations or work their charms to get rid of demons. Sometimes people sacrificed infants or made their children walk through fire.

People who wanted to be especially favored by the gods did even more. Priests initiated them through many rites and sacrifices and made them take vows of secrecy. When they were considered pure enough they could participate in a drama of death and resurrection such as the bull rite. For this, they descended into a pit under a platform where a bull was slaughtered. They let its blood drip over them until all their garments were saturated, and they turned up their faces so blood might trickle everywhere and they could get some on their tongues and drink it. Then they ascended from the pit and were greeted by priests and others who believed with them that they were now ready for eternity. Or at least this baptism would last for twenty years.

The skin of a black bull was stretched and made into a drum, and when the sacred drum was beat, worshipers danced and chanted and cut themselves. All of life revolved around the gods in Babel and the other cities, each of which had its own priest-king and temples full of other priests and priestesses.

People brought offerings to the temples like taxes; it was required. So clerks needed to write how much barley or how many sheep a man brought. Without records, they would not know who had paid his taxes and who had not.

But after the disaster of the tower of Bel, people could not write in their new languages. They had only a dim memory of the old symbols which gave both sounds and meanings. If someone remembered how to write the meaning of a word, it didn't fit the sound. Or if he remembered how to write a sound, it didn't fit the meaning he wanted.

So at first they made pictures to stand for barley and sheep and other ideas that they needed. These pictures, called ideograms, became useful for writing sounds, too, even if the sounds had a different meaning. Thus *ga*, or milk, could be used for the sound *ga* in any word, even where it didn't mean milk. People liked the sound system because it kept the list of ideograms from becoming too long.

To make writing easier to teach in their temple schools, men changed the pictures into simplified symbols. To make it faster, they stylized each symbol. Eventually, they formed all their symbols with combinations of wedge-shaped marks. Then they could simply press into soft clay a stylus which made wedge-shaped marks for them.

Thus in a short time, the priests and their pupils were writing again. Accountants kept track of temple business and the king's business.

Down the rivers, in the cities of the dark-headed people, they called their language Sumerian. This language had changed more than others during the disaster, and it was not at all like languages around them. Nevertheless, tradesmen there managed to learn the language of Babel so they could trade with those people to their north.

Boys in Sumerian schools studied dictionary tablets with Sumerian words listed down one side of a line and the corresponding Babylonian words listed on the other side of the line. School was hard and boring for those boys. They were only allowed three days each month for time off from studies. They memorized a calendar poem and chanted about the three days off, and three days for festivals of the gods, and twenty-four days each month for school. "They are long days," wrote a pupil on his tablet when the teacher wasn't looking. Besides languages, the boys studied drawing and arithmetic and geometry.

Once people could write again, some of them began to write poetry and history. In Sumer, each city wanted its history to look longer than anyone else's history. That rivalry started with the king of Kish. He conquered other cities and then called himself the Big King. After the Flood, he said, kingship was sent down from on high to him in Kish. But other rulers wanted to become Big Kings, so wars began among the cities, each one trying to rule the others.

In Erech, the ruler said that kingship was sent down from on high to Erech, moved there from Kish. If he included Kish's kings in a list before his own kingship, it gave him a longer history to uphold his claim to divine kingship. Then rulers in Ur, which was down the river from Erech, claimed the same thing.

So cities in Sumer kept lists and claimed long histories. Some old men said, "That first king reigned 1200 years," or "This king reigned 1500 years." People used to have long lives, they explained. And so the histories grew longer.

"Why not write the history of kings before the Flood?" some one asked one day. Did anyone have a list? Did any old men remember?

Some did remember dimly what they had learned in childhood,

but since the language disaster it was hard to come up with those names. There were ten kings, someone recalled. No, said another. There were only eight, because two of the fathers outlived their sons, so you can't count those sons in the list. They argued and some people wrote an eight-king list and others wrote a ten-king list. No one wrote a name like Adam or Seth in their lists, but they did the best they could.

Kings reigned a very long time before the Flood, the old men said. The first king, they thought, reigned for 8 sars, which was a very long time, indeed. Some of the others reigned as long as 10 or 12 sars. Their cities? Arguments started again, and people confused cities before the Flood with cities after the Flood as though they were the same ones rebuilt.

Some historians were poets. They wrote poem-stories of how the world began and how the Flood came, the two most important events in their history.

First there was only Sea, the stories said, vast ocean that was never created but always was, eternal ocean. Sea gave birth to Heaven-Earth. Heaven-Earth then gave birth to Air, which expanded between them and separated Heaven from Earth. The heaven god carried off Heaven and the air god, Enlil, carried off his mother Earth. After that, Enlil begat more gods and he was the most powerful of them all.

"No!" some old men objected when they heard what young boys were learning at school. Sea was not first. That's the way Nimrod's priests heard it from the god of the air. And earth was not a mother. It was the other way around; the gods created earth and sea. In fact, wasn't it one eternal God who created all things?

But the priests taught it their way. They controlled the schools.

Boys learned of the battle of the gods in which the dragon of the abyss, named Kur, is slain. The priest-poet in one city wrote the story a bit differently from the priest-poet in another city, so stories about this battle varied from city to city. So, too, did the other stories vary—those which told about the gifts of civilization and wisdom which the gods gave to man.

Poem-stories of the Great Flood were mixed up too. Writers forgot the name of Noah, and thought his name was Ziusudra. Stories related how a god spoke to him through a wall and said the gods were planning to destroy the earth. He should build a boat, the god told him, and take the seed of all living things into it.

What would happen when neighbors saw him building a boat?

He should tell them that the gods doomed him to go dwell in the Deep, but the gods will shower blessings upon them. The neighbors were deceived, and when rain started they thought it was blessings from the gods. One god thundered. Another tore down the doorposts of gates that held back the waters of the upper ocean. Another lifted up torches so that the land was ablaze with their glare. On the seventh day the raging storm ceased and all mankind had returned to clay. Ziusudra sent out a dove and a swallow and they returned. Then he sent out a raven and it did not return, so he let all living things out from the ship and offered sacrifice to the gods. The high goddess lifted up her necklace of lapis lazuli and promised that this would never happen again.

A story of Adapa, whose name sounded a little like Adam, told of this first man going up to the god of heaven where he refused the bread and water of life but accepted a garment and anointing oil, just as the god of wisdom had advised him to do. The god of heaven laughed and said, "Because you refused the bread and water, you will not have the gift of immortality."

Heroes in tale after tale stormed heaven and earth and the underworld in search of that gift of immortality. They crossed mountains, slew dragons, braved deadly waters, fought against the gods and for the gods, tricked the gods, placated them, and begged and stole trees of life. But nothing worked.

In the end, this is what happens to a man:

The god turned me into a ghost,
So that my arms were like those of a bird.
Looking at me, he leads me to the House of Darkness,
The abode of Irkalla,
To the house which none leave who have entered it,
On the road from which there is no way back,
To the house wherein the dwellers are bereft of light,
Where dust is their fare and clay their food.
They are clothed like birds, with wings for garments,
And see no light, residing in darkness.

18. The Death of Noah

When Noah was 950 years old he died. Shem sent for his two brothers to come home and join him in the burial of their father. Japheth in Hellas and Ham in Mizraim both had a considerable distance to travel, but they came.

Old animosities were mellowed now, and when the brothers came together they arranged a suitable monument for Noah's burial place and planned a memorial service in his honor. A crowd of people attended. People living near Mount Ararat held Noah in utmost reverence. They valued the knowledge of mankind's history, and Noah had been a living vestige of much of that history. Many in the crowd also revered the God who created the world and who had judged it with so complete a judgment as the Flood. The Flood seemed almost a part of their own memories because of Noah living in their midst and because of the ark, which to this day lodged near the mountaintop, and which practically every man had seen as a schoolboy when he climbed with a group to view it.

But now Noah was gone. An era had passed. Everyone felt an acute loss.

A funeral was a rare event in the lives of Noah's friends. No one they knew had ever died of old age except for Noah's wife. They remembered a few deaths by drowning or hunting accidents. And one man had fallen to his death in a construction accident. Araratians had heard of killings and violence down on the plain to the south, but life had been more peaceful in their area.

Unaccustomed as they were to occasions like this, they sat hushed and solemn in the presence of the mystery of death.

Shem spoke more eloquently than ever, his voice full of emotion, his thoughts about God and man clear and penetrating. He retold the life of Noah, how he alone of all the old world found grace in the eyes of God, how he did all that God told him to do, how he and his family were saved through the Great Flood, and how he received the covenant from God for the new world. Shem's voice thundered out strong reminders of how his listeners should live. They should remember the coming Redeemer, the Ark of safety for all mankind. They should believe God as Noah did, and be saved from God's judgment upon sin.

Many listeners resolved in their hearts to live more like Noah. Japheth listened with amazement to his brother whom he hadn't heard for a long, long time. He liked everything Shem said, and he resolved to live more like Shem. When he returned to the lands where his descendants lived he would teach people once again the truth about God. So many these days didn't know the truth or didn't believe the truth anymore. Would the young generations listen to him now? Japheth realized, sadly, that he couldn't teach like Shem because he hadn't lived so faithful a life as Shem.

Ham bottled up more emotions inside him than anyone in the crowded assembly. He relived the years of building the ark and the traumatic year of the Great Flood. Tears welled up in his eyes when he thought of those tranquil years when his children were young and growing up happily with their cousins under the shadow of the mountain, which on this day stood before him seeming to preach like Shem, reminding him how powerful God is and how puny men are.

Thoughts crowded into Ham's mind about his children. Why hadn't he been more careful in teaching them? If he had known in those peaceful years what he knew now, would he have been a different kind of father? Such questions were too painful. He pushed them out as fast as they appeared.

The memorial service ended, and a large gathering of extended family members supped together afterward. For several days, groups talked hour after hour about the old days.

Gradually, families dispersed to their own homes, and at last Japheth, Shem and Ham had time to talk with each other privately. They did not speak their deepest feelings. They felt like little boys, playing together and working with their father. Again, they felt like young fathers playing with their own children. Did they really have great-great-grandchildren and further descendants numbering many thousands? Had the world gone through such cataclysmic changes as their memories told them?

Yes, of course, it all had happened. There they sat, the three oldest living men, the last remaining links with the old world. What had they done with their new world? It was too much for them to discuss in their emotionally exhausted condition. They dealt first with the present and took care of the business of Noah's estate.

Then Shem, considerate of his brothers' feelings, brought up the subject of the family history. He had long been preserving the books and collecting information about births and deaths in the families, but now he proposed that the three of them together decide what should be entered into the family history to follow Noah's section. "What should we include?" he asked.

"Let's hear once again the words already in the book," suggested Japheth.

Shem read aloud the words so familiar to them all. In childhood they had memorized, "In the beginning God created the heaven and the earth," and on down through the whole section that God had given to Adam, and then Adam's section about the garden, the serpent, and Cain and Abel. Shem didn't need the book, but to hide the tears in his eyes he looked at the words as he said them.

Japheth's memory for the words was returning, and he could almost quote them along with Shem. Ham had not thought about the words for a long time, but he too could quote parts as though he were standing at his father's knee.

The Death of Noah

Then they came to Noah's section. "Someone else's turn," said Shem. And Japheth volunteered. He read through the genealogy information that the old world patriarchs had passed down from one to another until it came to the hands and pen of Noah. This was the part the brothers remembered laboring so hard over as they taught their own children.

Last, came the all-too-brief section about wickedness in the old world and God's decision to destroy it. The room itself seemed heavy with emotion as Japheth read those words written by their recently buried father. Controlling his voice, he managed to finish it, reading, "But Noah found grace in the eyes of the Lord. This is the written account of Noah."

The three brothers were silent for a long time. At last one said, "We need to tell more about preparing for the Great Flood. And about the Flood year—people will want to know that."

Another added, "And we should tell more about our father. He was entirely too modest in writing about himself."

They pored over Shem's books for a time, selecting portions of his writings and of the log they had kept on the boat. They spent a few moments on the touchy subject of Noah's prophecies—the blessings and cursing on the three branches of the human family. They all knew it was important for mankind's history, and Ham had seen enough of that history by now that he admitted to himself the truth of the words. His brothers said no more than they had to about this part of the writings.

Feeling that their work was finished for the day, they refreshed themselves with some food and drink and retired for the night. The next day, Shem carefully wrote the account as the brothers had planned it. Then, together, they read it over.

They agreed upon the words as Shem had written them, so they closed the story with the signature which had become customary in the history: "This is the written account of the sons of Noah—Shem, Ham, and Japheth."

Their work done, the brothers talked in a more relaxed manner.

JAVAN
(GREECE)
BLACK SEA
HATTI
GREAT SEA
CRETE
SIDON
MEMPHIS
SINAI
PHUT
(LYBIA)
MIZRAIM
(EGYPT)
NILE RIVER
RED SEA
CUSH
(ETHIOPIA)

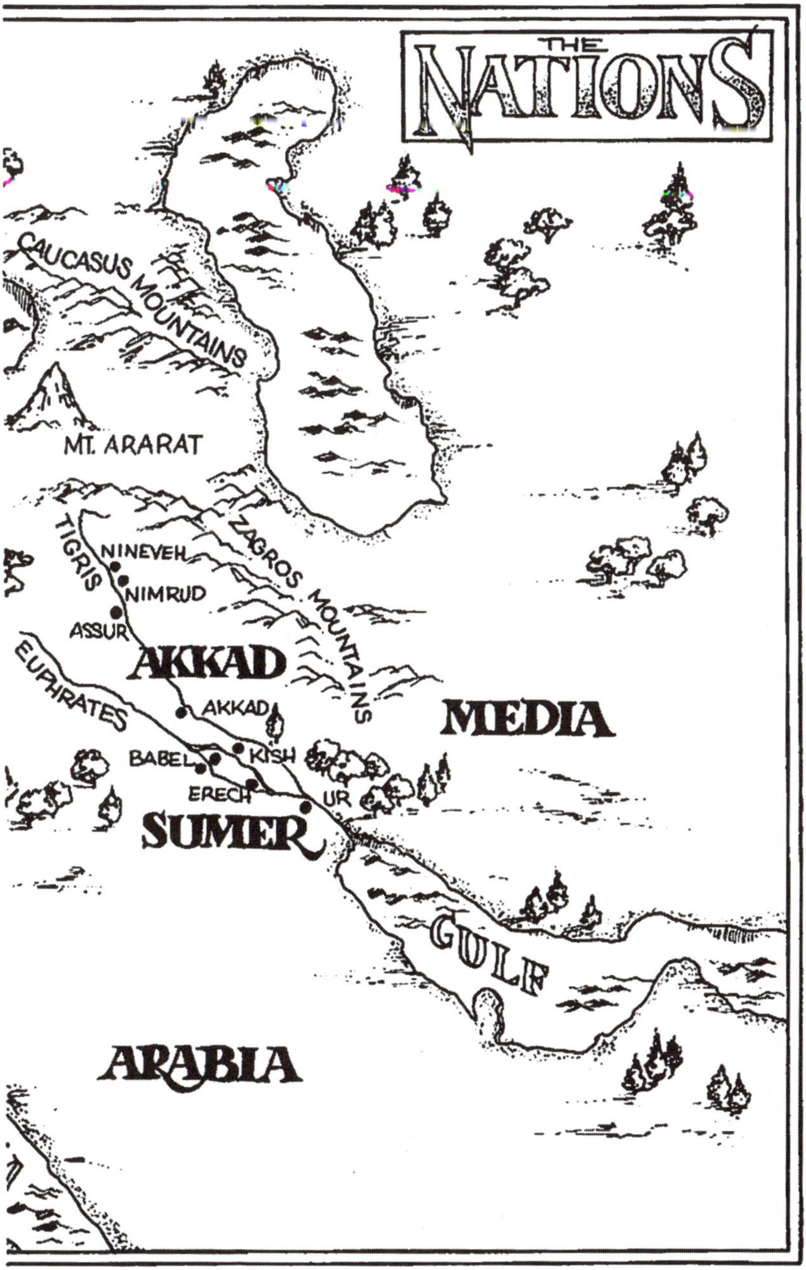
THE NATIONS
CAUCASUS MOUNTAINS
MT. ARARAT
TIGRIS
NINEVEH
NIMRUD
ASSUR
ZAGROS MOUNTAINS
AKKAD
EUPHRATES
AKKAD
MEDIA
BABEL
KISH
ERECH
UR
SUMER
GULF
ARABIA

The world was certainly changing these days, they commented. Shem looked at his collection of births and deaths and read bits of information to his brothers. One line of his offspring was listed down through Peleg and his brother Joktan. Peleg died at the young age of 239, and Shem had no further information about that branch of the family. They lived a nomadic life. He had visited often in Arabia, though, and knew all the sons of Joktan, and some of them had died before the age of 150. Men didn't inherit longevity anymore. Could the nova have caused this? Or the colder atmosphere? Or earthquakes and tidal waves and other physical events? They mentioned most of the theories that men were talking about. "If it is from the environment," said one, "we must remember the greatest change is that the sky fell during the Flood."

With a little shock the three men remembered. They tried to bring to mind that world of their youth, but the images were dim. They tried to compare today's harsh sunlight with the way it used to be, a warm glow filtering through the water above the sky. Perhaps the sun's direct rays were not good for man's health.

Their talk turned to political events of the nations they knew about. Ham told of the south where his son Menes ruled over an empire that he had earned the hard way. He was sometimes known by the name Mizraim, as were the land and its people, too. The name Mizraim meant "the embanker of the sea." The embanker's fame extended far, so that both Shem and Japheth had heard of this ruler. Shem jotted a notation in one of his books that Menes was Mizraim.

Ham explained how in the early days he and Menes had crossed the Red Sea into that vast continent that lay to its west, and settled along the Nile River. They found greener pastures there than in Arabia, which was becoming more arid all the time. As settlements proliferated, Menes cast his eye on the lower portions of the river. He saw the river washing across low land right up to the foothills of the Lybian Mountains on the west, which marked the beginning of territory claimed by his brother Phut. The descendants

The Death of Noah

of another brother, Cush, were south of him in a land called either Cush or Ethiopia. So if he wanted to enlarge his empire, the best direction was north down the river.

Menes realized that because the Great Sea had receded, much marsh land could be claimed and livable if the river were channeled properly. He needed only to divert the course of the Nile, to force it to run in a channel down the center of the valley and halt its waters spreading outward to the mountains.

Ham proudly recounted how Menes engineered a dyke project and diverted the river eastward. Then in a gesture of victory, he built the town of Memphis on the west bank where the river had formerly run. More communities sprang up on other sites of land reclaimed from water. Guards were stationed at all times to watch over the embankments and keep them in good repair.

The vigorous leader Menes united the lower settlements with those on the upper reaches of the river, and brought the whole land of Mizraim under his rule. He was called the Great House, the Pharaoh, of that land.

Japheth commented on how three of Ham's sons, Menes, Phut and Cush, had become neighboring nations on the southern continent. Shem asked about the sons of Menes, and he wrote the name of each one who had grown to become a tribe. Some tribes had trekked out to other parts of the vast continent and Ham did not know where they all were at this time. Casluhim and Caphtorim were boat builders, having learned some of their skills from Grandfather Ham himself, and they settled on the island of Crete in the Great Sea.

Ham's brothers delicately avoided mentioning Cush's son Nimrod, but they asked about the offspring of Ham's fourth son Canaan. Most of Canaan's many sons had settled along the shores of the Great Sea, and Shem completed his list of those tribes from information that Ham gave him. The tribe of Sidon had a good seaport. They built ships and plied the seas even more than Menes' sons on Crete, sailing afar and planting colonies wherever they found metals or ivory or other valuable commodities. They visited their colonies regularly for cargo, and carried on sea trade wherever their ships could go.

The southernmost tribe were the Sinites. They were not sea people, but were spreading southward onto a peninsula called by their name, the Sinai Peninsula.

The brothers congratulated Ham for knowing so much about his grandsons and their tribes. Ham explained that he learned a lot through the merchants of Mizraim. They did a brisk business with the Sidonians, and the Sidonian sea merchants were always full of news.

Japheth now took a turn telling about his offspring. He had been living west of practically everybody else, on the northern coasts of the Great Sea, with his son Javan and grandson Elishah, who now headed up a growing tribe called the Elishians, or sometimes the Hellenists. Japheth could name the other sons of Javan for Shem to list in his book. They were spreading westward along the Great Sea and some of its islands. He also knew who the sons of Gomer were. They had gone north of the Black Sea and explored and even settled up the rivers that flowed into it.

Some of Japheth's other sons were in the north, too, but he had lost track of their descendants. Vast fields of ice kept them from migrating very far north. That much he knew. Japheth's son Madai headed a growing tribe called the Medes in the east. Shem updated his list of Japhethites as much as he could with the information from Japheth.

Ham and Japheth began making preparations to return to their homes. The brothers remarked that they should see each other more often, but in their hearts they knew that this was probably the last time they would meet on earth. They felt that once they returned to their separate lives and lands, there would never be another event like their father's death to bring them together again. Shem's life of preaching was a problem to the other two; they knew his message was truth and they had done so poorly with truth in their own lands.

The goodbyes were cordial but restrained on the outside, while deep emotion stirred inside each man. Shem watched the two caravans leave, one after the other, and he stood a long time lost in thought, the weight of a world upon his shoulders.

19. Abram

After his father's death, Shem went to live among the sons of Joktan in Arabia. These sons were five generations after Shem, and their children and grandchildren were further removed yet, so that Shem seemed a solitary figure in their midst. Over 450 years old, he was the ancient grandfather, older than any man would ever be again, it seemed. People revered Shem but they did not know him well. A man of forty-five had little understanding of a man ten times as old.

With advancing age, Shem thought more often about the books in his care. In the history book he added his own section to follow what he and his brothers had inserted together. He listed first the descendants of Japheth, his elder brother, then the descendants of Ham, and then his own descendants as far as the thirteen sons of Joktan. He mentioned how the nations and tongues of mankind were divided according to these family groups.

Following that information about the family tree, Shem wrote of the apostasy at Babel and God's judgment upon it. He used the pattern set by Adam and Noah, of making as brief a story as possible when writing about the darkest hours of history. In only a few sentences he told of the rebellion at the tower at Babel and of God's judgment in confounding the languages and scattering people abroad on the earth.

Shem wrote in the language of Adam and Noah, the original Edenese, rather than the dialect of the tribe he lived among. The words had lost some of their original exactness and depth of meaning; people would not understand them as well as previously; but it was the best of the languages he knew and the proper language for writing this history of God's dealings with man.

Shem looked over his writing. Is that all he should say? Should he tell more about Nimrod? Should he mention the war against his preachers? Should he explain that the gods were really rebellious angels?

No, he decided. The account was just right the way it was. So he signed his manuscript with: "This is the written account of Shem." And he carefully stored it with the other books.

In the tribe where he was living, Shem considered each young man. Should he entrust the books to one of them? So far he hadn't found the right man. Perhaps someday God would reveal to him who would be the forefather of the promised Seed. If that happened he could be at peace about the books, knowing he was placing them in good hands.

Shem searched among the other Joktan tribes. He asked questions about who was worshiping God. He also traveled a little, not as much as in former days, but he sometimes made his way as far as the always-warring towns in Sumer. He spoke some of the languages and he used interpreters for others. Everywhere, he was received as a legend, as someone more than a man.

Once he considered a man named Job who lived quite a distance from him, over in the land of Uz. The fame of Job had spread far, especially after certain calamities befell him. It seemed he lost all his cattle and their herders to invaders. Then lightning struck his sheep and the shepherds. And so it went, with more invaders and more violent weather taking all that Job had, including his family. Everyone who told the story agreed that Job did not deserve such a fate. He was a righteous man, they said, who made offerings to God continually. He was a respected man among princes and rulers.

A traveler passed through Shem's village on his way to visit

Job. "I am meeting two other friends," he said, "and we are going to mourn with Job and comfort him."

Was Job the man Shem was searching for? Perhaps. He would wait and see.

Later, on one of his travels, he heard that God had appeared to a man in Ur. As far as he knew, the last time God appeared to anyone was to Adam in the garden. And now Ur, of all places! That town held on to the evils of Babel more than any town in the world. Surely someone was confused and was referring to a pagan god instead of Shem's God.

But something about the story drew him to investigate. In the old world God found one righteous man, Noah. Maybe God was doing this again. Shem made his way to Ur.

As he approached the city from the south, Shem could see on its left the temple of the mother goddess. The morning sun reflected from the copper and milky pearl of the shrine, which Shem loathed in his heart, but which stood high on a platform so he could not avoid seeing it. Even from his distance, Shem saw the gleaming copper lion heads flanking the entrance at the top of the stairway and the copper bulls adorning the walls of the platform below. How ignorant men had become, thought Shem, and how few there are who accept the truth in these days.

Straight ahead, in the center of the city itself, was an even higher tower. Only a fraction of the height of the tower of Bel, it nevertheless rose above its surrounding walls and cast a shadow across the morning. Its series of platforms, one atop the other, resembled that other tower in architecture and extravagant embellishments. A shrine to Nanna the moon god, the god of Ur, stood on its highest platform, glowing as blue as the morning sky.

Shem tried to shake off thoughts of the abominations enacted there daily. Had God spoken to a man living under the shadows of Ur?

Shem entered the city and was directed to the house of a man named Terah. Passing through the streets, he observed more of the

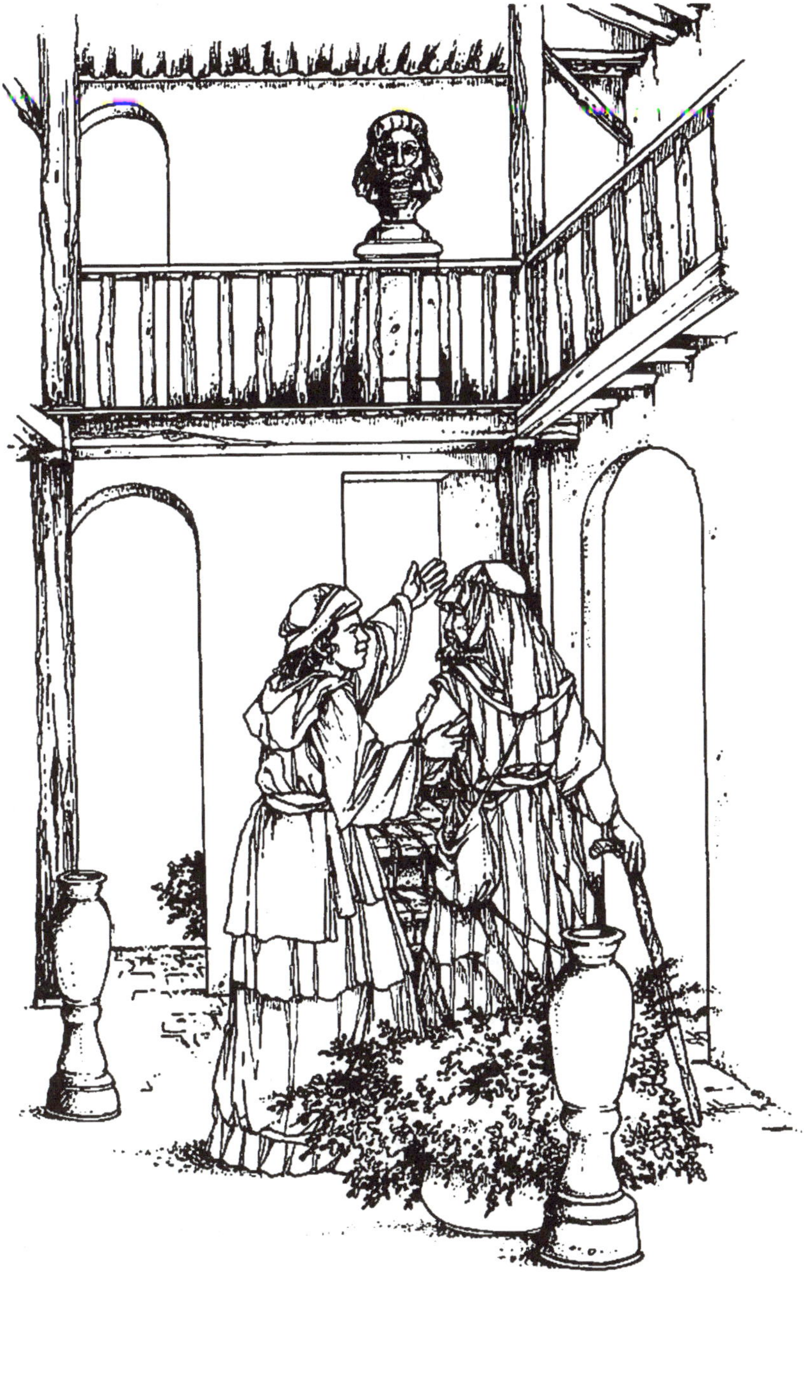

fabulous wealth of the city. Temples to lesser gods than Nanna were not built as high, but they, too, were elaborately ornamented and were centers of activity, with people constantly coming and going with animals and carts of produce.

Turning away from the city center, Shem passed along a narrow street lined with homes. Between the houses, in every available space, were small chapels to more gods, and people were availing themselves of these also, bringing offerings to the small images and asking favors of the gods.

The house Shem sought was three stories high and appeared to belong to a wealthy man. A servant led him through the arched doorway and into an open courtyard. Here he waited a few moments, taking pleasure in the cool air and quiet surroundings. Looking up past the rooms and balconies of the upper levels, he could see a bit of sky, but the hot sun did not shine down on him. Soon he was led past a chapel, where, to his dismay, he saw family idols, and on to a guest chamber.

After he refreshed himself, he at last met Terah. With knowledge of Terah's idols in the back of his mind, he cautiously began to talk with him about the call of God that he heard of in his own land.

Yes, said Terah, God had appeared to his son Abram and told him to leave this country and go to a land that God would show him. God promised to make of him a great nation, which would be a blessing to the world.

In those words Shem heard echoes of his own father's prophecy. Was Terah a Shemite and a potential ancestor of the Seed? Terah brought out for Shem his family genealogy. Shem saw immediately that it was written in Edenese and not in the awkward Sumerian cuneiform he had expected.

Shem mentioned this, and Terah switched to the language of his father and grandfathers. When with his nomadic tribesmen he spoke that tongue, he explained. But now he was in the business of cattle trading and spent much of his time in town, and he used

Sumerian here. The family called their language Ebru after an ancestor named Eber.

As Shem listened to him speak, he marveled because Terah's language was even closer to the original Edenese than the dialects he knew among Joktan's descendants. And the genealogy, too, was almost pure Edenese.

Shem studied the document closely. The genealogy started at the Great Flood, because all families liked to show how directly they were descended from the original survivors of the Flood. Thus it began with Shem's own name. It proceeded through Shem's son Arphaxad down the generations to Eber. Then it followed Peleg's branch instead of Joktan's branch. Terah was descended from Peleg, the brother of Joktan.

Shem was excited. Where was Abram? At the moment he was busy with preparations for their journey, Terah explained. There was much to be done, with flocks and servants and three households—his own and Abram's and that of a grandson Lot. Terah was convinced that God wanted his whole family to make the move.

Where would they go, Shem asked.

First they would go to Haran to settle the estate of Terah's son Haran who had just died here in Ur. Haran had come to help bury Terah's father, and then Haran himself had died rather suddenly. Shem extended his condolences to Terah upon hearing of this. He remembered burying his own father. He hadn't yet buried a son, but he knew two such losses in one year would be very hard on a family.

Was it these deaths which had stirred Terah to take his family to the land God would show them? It seemed so to Shem. Instead of the call of God moving him to action, the two deaths provided the push that Terah needed. Shem asked again about meeting Abram.

Terah was a gracious host and felt honored to have the legendary Shem in his home. He directed his servants to bring food and to take care of every need of Shem's until Abram could be brought. But Shem declined to eat. "I will stand here and wait," he said.

Immediately upon meeting Abram, Shem knew he had found the man he was looking for. He asked Abram about God's appearance, and listened intently to the story. Then Abram asked Shem what he knew about ancient oracles of God.

When Shem began talking, it seemed that he knew everything. Abram asked question after question, about the Flood and Noah, about stars, about God. Did Shem have these things written in books?

Abram and Terah had heard there were true books somewhere. In the Ur library they had seen stories of Creation, of the Great Flood and other old-time events, but they knew in their hearts that the stories were corrupted, as was all literature in the Sumerian language. Their pastoral forefathers told another version, and they knew that their family used to have some of those stories in books. But nomadic herdsmen don't keep books very well. They had managed somehow to hold on only to the genealogy.

God preserved that genealogy for them, exclaimed Shem. Then he told about his books, how they were passed down from Adam and the old world patriarchs until they reached Noah, and how Shem and his brothers added their manuscripts to the history. Now it needed Terah's genealogy to bring it up to date.

Then Shem began to tell the story in the books, the straight, uncorrupted story. He began at the beginning, telling how God created heaven and earth, how Adam sinned and death came into the world, how God first promised the Seed which would conquer death and evil once and for all.

Terah and Abram listened with rapt attention as Shem continued with the story. He came to Noah's prophecy about blessing the Lord God of Shem, and it seemed an echo of that first promise from God.

Now here sat Terah and Abram, descendants of Shem, and

Abram 133

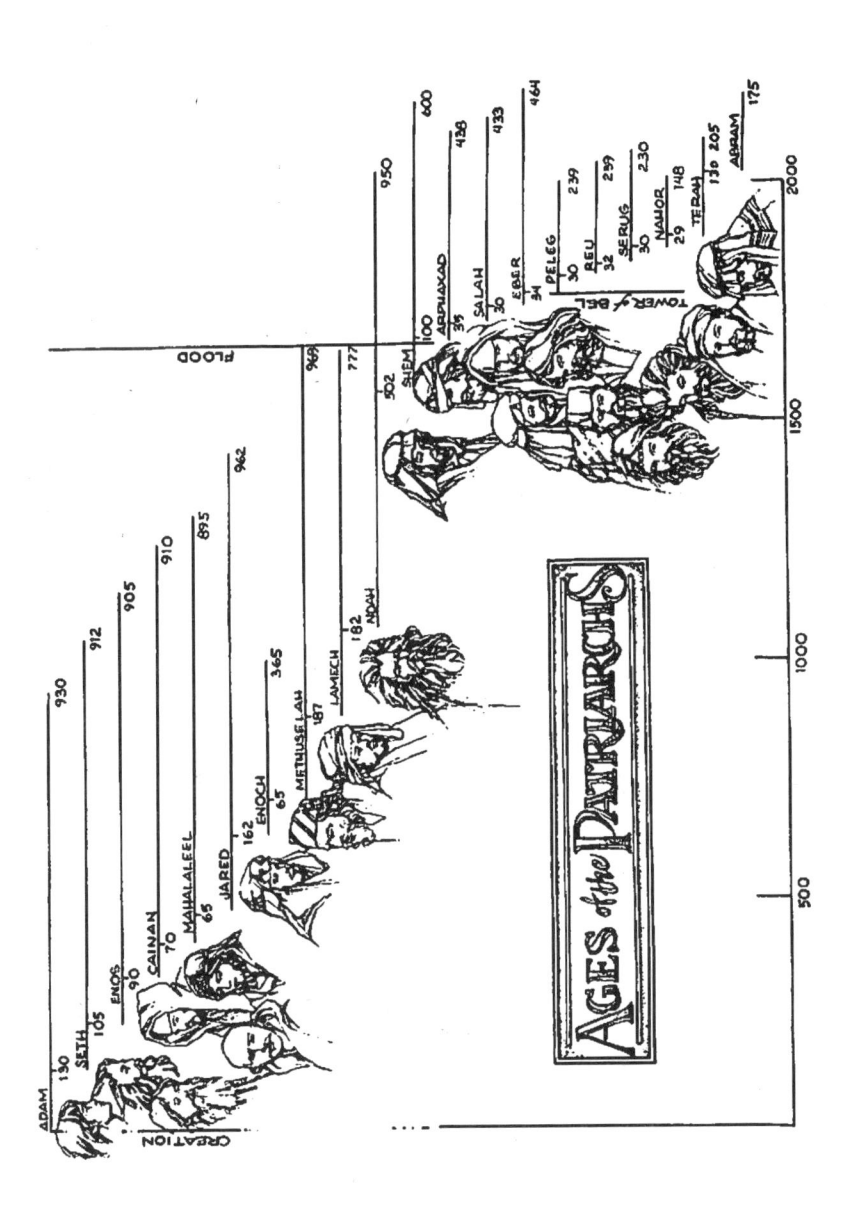

God had spoken again to them. The Seed line is preserved. God remembered his promise.

"I don't even have a son yet," said Abram.

"Perhaps God is waiting until you are in the land," said Shem. "Obey God; then watch Him fulfill His promise to make of you a great nation."

Shem desired now to entrust the books to Terah and Abram. Yes, they said, they would guard the books.

After a few days, Shem prepared to return home. Terah instructed several of his most trusted servants to accompany him and to bring back the valuable books. Abram, his heart full from the events of this visit and of the responsibility and uncertainty of the future, embraced Shem. The aged Shem spoke blessings upon Abram as upon a beloved son. After embracings and goodbyes, Shem departed. Abram watched until the little caravan disappeared from view.

With vigor, Terah returned to preparations for his own journey. Yes, they must go, he realized. He cannot delay any longer.

In a few days the servants returned with the books and Terah read the history. Being inexperienced at book writing, he wanted to see how the others had done it. He noticed the part that said Noah was 500 years old and "begat Shem, Ham, and Japheth."

The three sons were combined in one sentence without mentioning who was oldest or intimating who was chosen of God.

That's what he would do, he decided. So after the list of his grandfathers he added the birth of his own sons, saying, "And Terah lived seventy years, and begat Abram, Nahor, and Haran." He didn't say who was the oldest. He didn't mention that Haran had died or that Abram was chosen of God or that Nahor would not be accompanying them to the promised land. He just listed them according to the pattern Noah had set and Shem had followed.

He also noticed that Noah's list included how long each patriarch lived after the birth of the son mentioned. Terah could not do that on his list because all his ancestors on this side of the Great Flood were still living, except for Peleg and for his own father who died at only 148 years of age. "Abram will have to insert that information someday," thought Terah. Then he added ruefully, "If he lives long enough." The way people were dying these days, he could see that the life span wasn't what it used to be.

So Terah was finished. He signed the genealogy according to the pattern set by his predecessors:

> This is the written account of Terah.

He carefully packed his manuscript and loaded it in a cart with the other books. Then he packed his idols, which were almost the last remaining items in his house. On the morrow they would leave.

A far larger caravan than Shem's began the journey north. They would be traveling through the prosperous, fertile lands of Sumer and Akkad, through several of their wealthy, warring, pagan towns, through Babel itself, the mother of them all, on to Haran near the mountains of the north. From there the plan was to go to the land that God would show them.

Appendix A
Writers of Genesis

Dr. Henry M. Morris has suggested a division of the early portions of Genesis according to which patriarch wrote each portion (*The Genesis Record*, Baker Book House, 1976). Upon examination, this system seems reasonable. The Hebrew word *toledoth* appears between each division, and it translates into English "generations," or "origins." By extension, the whole statement means, "This is the record of the generations of . . . ." And by inference it could mean, "This is the written record of the generations of . . . ." For concreteness and clarity this latter form is used in this book.

The key to seeing this pattern in Genesis is to realize that the toledoths come at the end of a man's writing instead of at the beginning, as the verse divisions, and even chapter divisions, make them appear. One can see that in every man's case except Terah's the writer who signed off with a toledoth could know the information preceding the signature, but not that which follows.

In Terah's section, the problem is the death age of several of his ancestors. If we take the chronology literally, these outlived Terah, and some compiler such as Moses would have had to insert their ages of death at a later time. If a reader wants to suppose some extra generations between Terah and those particular ancestors, that would solve the problem, but would raise another problem of why generations were skipped in a genealogy otherwise so carefully kept.

Here is a list of writers, according to toledoth divisions of the portions of Genesis covered in this book.
1. Lord God (or God gave to Adam)—to Genesis 2:4.
2. Adam—to Genesis 5:1.
3. Noah—to Genesis 6:9.
4. The sons of Noah—to Genesis 10:1.
5. Shem—to Genesis 11:10.
6. Terah—to Genesis 11:27.

In Appendix B this portion of Genesis is given in the King James Version with these divisions.

Appendix B
Genesis 1:1 to 11:27a

God's Book of the
Creation of the Heavens and Earth

1:1 In the beginning God created the heaven and the earth.

2 And the earth was without form, and void; and darkness *was* upon the face of the deep. And the Spirit of God moved upon the face of the waters.

3 And God said, Let there be light: and there was light.

4 And God saw the light, that *it was* good: and God divided the light from the darkness.

5 And God called the light Day, and the darkness he called Night. And the evening and the morning were the first day.

6 And God said, Let there be a firmament in the midst of the waters, and let it divide the waters from the waters.

7 And God made the firmament, and divided the waters which *were* under the firmament from the waters which *were* above the firmament: and it was so.

8 And God called the firmament Heaven. And the evening and the morning were the second day.

9 And God said, Let the waters under the heaven be gathered together unto one place, and let the dry *land* appear: and it was so.

10 And God called the dry *land* Earth; and the gathering together of the waters called he Seas: and God saw that it *was* good.

11 And God said, Let the earth bring forth grass, the herb yielding seed, *and* the fruit tree yielding fruit after his kind, whose seed *is* in itself, upon the earth: and it was so.

12 And the earth brought forth grass, *and* herb yielding seed after his kind, and the tree yielding fruit, whose seed *was* in itself, after his kind: and God saw that *it was* good.

13 And the evening and the morning were the third day.

14 And God said. Let there be lights in the firmament of the heaven to divide the day from the night; and let them be for signs, and for seasons, and for days, and years:

15 And let them be for lights in the firmament of the heaven to give light upon the earth: and it was so.

16 And God made two great lights; the greater light to rule the day, and the lesser light to rule the night: *he made* the stars also.

17 And God set them in the firmament of the heaven to give light upon the earth,

18 And to rule over the day and over the night, and to divide the light from the darkness: and God saw that *it was* good.

19 And the evening and the morning were the fourth day.

20 And God said, Let the waters bring forth abundantly the moving creature that hath life, and fowl *that* may fly above the earth in the open firmament of heaven.

21 And God created great whales, and every living creature that moveth, which the waters brought forth abundantly, after their kind, and every winged fowl after his kind: and God saw that *it was* good.

22 And God blessed them, saying, Be fruitful, and multiply, and fill the waters in the seas, and let fowl multiply in the earth.

23 And the evening and the morning were the fifth day.

24 And God said, Let the earth bring forth the living creature after his kind, cattle, and creeping thing, and beast of the earth after his kind: and it was so.

25 And God made the beast of the earth after his kind, and cattle after their kind, and every thing that creepeth upon the earth after his kind: and God saw that *it was* good.

26 And God said, Let us make man in our image, after our likeness: and let them have dominion over the fish of the sea, and over the fowl of the air, and over the cattle, and over all the earth, and over every creeping thing that creepeth upon the earth.

27 So God created man in his *own* image, in the image of God created he him; male and female created he them.

28 And God blessed them, and God said unto them, Be fruitful, and multiply, and replenish the earth, and subdue it: and have dominion over the fish of the sea, and over the fowl of the air, and over every living thing that moveth upon the earth.

29 And God said, Behold, I have given you every herb bearing seed, which *is* upon the face of all the earth, and every tree, in the which *is* the fruit of a tree yielding seed; to you it shall be for meat.

30 And to every beast of the earth, and to every fowl of the air, and to every thing that creepeth upon the earth, wherein *there is* life, *I have given* every green herb for meat: and it was so.

31 And God saw every thing that he had made, and, behold, *it was* very good. And the evening and the morning were the sixth day.

2:1 Thus the heavens and the earth were finished, and all the host of them.

2 And on the seventh day God ended his work which he had made; and he rested on the seventh day from all his work which he had made.

3 And God blessed the seventh day, and sanctified it: because that in it he had rested from all his work which God created and made.

4a These *are* the generations of the heavens and of the earth when they were created . . .

Appendix B

Book of Adam

4b . . . in the day that the Lord God made the earth and the heavens,

5 And every plant of the field before it was in the earth, and every herb of the field before it grew: for the Lord God had not caused it to rain upon the earth, and *there was* not a man to till the ground.

6 But there went up a mist from the earth, and watered the whole face of the ground.

7 And the LORD God formed man *of* the dust of the ground, and breathed into his nostrils the breath of life; and man became a living soul.

8 And the LORD God planted a garden eastward in Eden; and there he put the man whom he had formed.

9 And out of the ground made the LORD God to grow every tree that is pleasant to the sight, and good for food; the tree of life also in the midst of the garden, and the tree of knowledge of good and evil.

10 And a river went out of Eden to water the garden; and from thence it was parted, and became into four heads.

11 The name of the first *is* Pison: that *is* it which compasseth the whole land of Havilah, where *there is* gold;

12 And the gold of that land *is* good: there *is* bdellium and the onyx stone.

13 And the name of the second river *is* Gihon: the same *is* it that com passeth the whole land of Ethiopia.

14 And the name of the third river *is* Hiddekel: that *is* it which goeth toward the east of Assyria. And the fourth river *is* Euphrates.

15 And the LORD God took the man, and put him into the garden of Eden to dress it and to keep it.

16 And the Lord God commanded the man, saying. Of every tree of the garden thou mayest freely eat.

17 But of the tree of the knowledge of good and evil, thou shalt not eat of it: for in the day that thou eatest thereof thou shalt surely die.

18 And the LORD God said, *It is* not good that the man should be alone; I will make him an help meet for him.

19 And out of the ground the LORD God formed every beast of the field, and every fowl of the air; and brought *them* unto Adam to see what he would call them: and whatsoever Adam called every living creature, that *was* the name thereof.

20 And Adam gave names to all cattle, and to the fowl of the air, and to every beast of the field; but for Adam there was not found an help meet for him.

21 And the Lord God caused a deep sleep to fall upon Adam, and he slept: and he took one of his ribs, and closed up the flesh instead thereof;

22 And the rib, which the LORD God had taken from man, made he a woman, and brought her unto the man.

23 And Adam said, This *is* now bone of my bones, and flesh of my flesh: she shall be called Woman, because she was taken out of Man.

24 Therefore shall a man leave his father and his mother, and shall cleave unto his wife: and they shall be one flesh.

25 And they were both naked, the man and his wife, and were not ashamed.

3:1 Now the serpent was more subtil than any beast of the field which the LORD God had made. And he said unto the woman, Yea, hath God said, Ye shall not eat of every tree of the garden?

2 And the woman said unto the serpent,

We may eat of the fruit of the trees of the garden:

3 But of the fruit of the tree which *is* in the midst of the garden, God hath said, Ye shall not eat of it, neither shall ye touch it, lest ye die.

4 And the serpent said unto the woman, Ye shall not surely die:

5 For God doth know that in the day ye eat thereof, then your eyes shall be opened, and ye shall be as gods, knowing good and evil.

6 And when the woman saw that the tree *was* good for food, and that it *was* pleasant to the eyes, and a tree to be desired to make *one* wise, she took of the fruit thereof, and did eat, and gave also unto her husband with her; and he did eat.

7 And the eyes of them both were opened, and they knew that they *were* naked; and they sewed fig leaves together, and made themselves aprons.

8 And they heard the voice of the LORD God walking in the garden in the cool of the day: and Adam and his wife hid themselves from the presence of the Lord God amongst the trees of the garden.

9 And the LORD God called unto Adam, and said unto him, Where *art* thou?

10 And he said, I heard thy voice in the garden, and I was afraid, because I *was* naked; and I hid myself.

11 And he said, Who told thee that thou *wast* naked? Hast thou eaten of the tree, whereof I commanded thee that thou shouldest not eat?

12 And the man said, The woman whom thou gavest *to be* with me, she gave me of the tree, and I did eat.

13 And the Lord God said unto the woman, What *is* this *that* thou hast done? And the woman said, The serpent beguiled me, and I did eat.

14 And the LORD God said unto the serpent, Because thou hast done this, thou *art* cursed above all cattle, and above every beast of the field; upon thy belly shalt thou go, and dust shalt thou eat all the days of thy life:

15 And I will put enmity between thee and the woman, and between thy seed and her seed; it shall bruise thy head, and thou shalt bruise his heel.

16 Unto the woman he said, I will greatly multiply thy sorrow and thy conception; in sorrow thou shalt bring forth children; and thy desire *shall be* to thy husband, and he shall rule over thee.

17 And unto Adam he said, Because thou hast hearkened unto the voice of thy wife, and hast eaten of the tree, of which I commanded thee, saying, Thou shalt not eat of it: cursed *is* the ground for thy sake; in sorrow shalt thou eat *of* it all the days of thy life;

18 Thorns also and thistles shall it bring forth to thee; and thou shalt eat the herb of the field;

19 In the sweat of thy face shalt thou eat bread, till thou return unto the ground; for out of it wast thou taken: for dust thou *art*, and unto dust shalt thou return.

20 And Adam called his wife's name Eve; because she was the mother of all living.

21 Unto Adam also and to his wife did the LORD God make coats of skins, and clothed them.

22 And the Lord God said, Behold, the man is become as one of us, to know good and evil: and now, lest he put forth his hand, and take also of the tree of life, and eat, and live for ever:

23 Therefore the Lord God sent him forth from the garden of Eden, to till the

ground from whence he was taken.

24 So he drove out the man; and he placed at the east of the garden of Eden Cherubims, and a flaming sword which turned every way, to keep the way of the tree of life.

4:1 And Adam knew Eve his wife; and she conceived, and bare Cain, and said, I have gotten a man from the Lord.

2 And she again bare his brother Abel. And Abel was a keeper of sheep, but Cain was a tiller of the ground.

3 And in process of time it came to pass, that Cain brought of the fruit of the ground an offering unto the LORD.

4 And Abel, he also brought of the firstlings of his flock and of the fat thereof. And the LORD had respect unto Abel and to his offering:

5 But unto Cain and to his offering he had not respect. And Cain was very wroth, and his countenance fell.

6 And the LORD said unto Cain, Why art thou wroth? and why is thy countenance fallen?

7 If thou doest well, shalt thou not be accepted? and if thou doest not well, sin lieth at the door. And unto thee *shall be* his desire, and thou shalt rule over him.

8 And Cain talked with Abel his brother: and it came to pass, when they were in the field, that Cain rose up against Abel his brother, and slew him.

9 And the Lord said unto Cain, Where *is* Abel thy brother? And he said, I know not: *Am* I my brother's keeper?

10 And he said. What hast thou done? the voice of thy brother's blood crieth unto me from the ground.

11 And now *art* thou cursed from the earth, which hath opened her mouth to receive thy brother's blood from thy hand;

12 When thou tillest the ground, it shall not henceforth yield unto thee her strength; a fugitive and a vagabond shalt thou be in the earth.

13 And Cain said unto the LORD, My punishment *is* greater than I can bear.

14 Behold, thou hast driven me out this day from the face of the earth; and from thy face shall I be hid; and I shall be a fugitive and a vagabond in the earth; and it shall come to pass, *that* every one that findeth me shall slay me.

15 And the LORD said unto him, Therefore whosoever slayeth Cain, vengeance shall be taken on him sevenfold. And the Lord set a mark upon Cain, lest any finding him should kill him.

16 And Cain went out from the presence of the LORD, and dwelt in the land of Nod, on the east of Eden.

17 And Cain knew his wife; and she conceived, and bare Enoch: and he builded a city, and called the name of the city, after the name of his son, Enoch.

18 And unto Enoch was born Irad: and Irad begat Mehujael: and Mehujael begat Methusael: and Methusael begat Lamech.

19 And Lamech took unto him two wives: the name of the one *was* Adah, and the name of the other Zillah.

20 And Adah bare Jabal: he was the father of such as dwell in tents, and *of such as have* cattle.

21 And his brother's name *was* Jubal: he was the father of all such as handle the harp and organ.

22 And Zillah, she also bare Tubalcain, an instructer of every artificer in brass and iron: and the sister of Tubalcain *was* Naamah.

23 And Lamech said unto his wives, Adah and Zillah, Hear my voice; ye wives of Lamech, hearken unto my speech: for I have slain a man to my wounding, and a

young man to my hurt.

24 If Cain shall be avenged seven fold, truly Lamech seventy and sevenfold.

25 And Adam knew his wife again; and she bare a son, and called his name Seth: For God, *said she*, hath appointed me another seed instead of Abel, whom Cain slew.

26 And to Seth, to him also there was born a son; and he called his name Enos: then began men to call upon the name of the LORD.

5:1a This *is* the book of the generations of Adam.

Book of Noah

1b In the day that God created man, in the likeness of God made he him;

2 Male and female created he them; and blessed them, and called their name Adam, in the day when they were created.

3 And Adam lived an hundred and thirty years, and begat *a son* in his own likeness, after his image; and called his name Seth:

4 And the days of Adam after he had begotten Seth were eight hundred years: and he begat sons and daughters:

5 And all the days that Adam lived were nine hundred and thirty years: and he died.

6 And Seth lived an hundred and five years, and begat Enos:

7 And Seth lived after he begat Enos eight hundred and seven years, and begat sons and daughters:

8 And all the days of Seth were nine hundred and twelve years: and he died.

9 And Enos lived ninety years, and begat Cainan:

10 And Enos lived after he begat Cainan eight hundred and fifteen years, and begat sons and daughters:

11 And all the days of Enos were nine hundred and five years: and he died.

12 And Cainan lived seventy years, and begat Mahalaleel:

13 And Cainan lived after he begat Mahalaleel eight hundred and forty years, and begat sons and daughters:

14 And all the days of Cainan were nine hundred and ten years: and he died.

15 And Mahalaleel lived sixty and five years, and begat Jared:

16 And Mahalaleel lived after he begat Jared eight hundred and thirty years, and begat sons and daughters:

17 And all the days of Mahalaleel were eight hundred ninety and five years: and he died.

18 And Jared lived an hundred sixty and two years, and he begat Enoch:

19 And Jared lived after he begat Enoch eight hundred years, and begat sons and daughters:

20 And all the days of Jared were nine hundred sixty and two years: and he died.

21 And Enoch lived sixty and five years, and begat Methuselah:

22 And Enoch walked with God after he begat Methuselah three hundred years, and begat sons and daughters:

23 And all the days of Enoch were three hundred sixty and five years:

24 And Enoch walked with God: and he *was* not; for God took him.

25 And Methuselah lived an hundred eighty and seven years, and begat Lamech:

26 And Methuselah lived after he begat Lamech seven hundred eighty and two years, and begat sons and daughters:

Appendix B

27 And all the days of Methuselah were nine hundred sixty and nine years: and he died.

28 And Lamech lived an hundred eighty and two years, and begat a son:

29 And he called his name Noah, saying. This *same* shall comfort us concerning our work and toil of our hands, because of the ground which the LORD hath cursed.

30 And Lamech lived after he begat Noah five hundred ninety and Ave years, and begat sons and daughters:

31 And all the days of Lamech were seven hundred seventy and seven years: and he died.

32 And Noah was five hundred years old: and Noah begat Shem, Ham, and Japheth.

6:1 And it came to pass, when men began to multiply on the face of the earth, and daughters were born unto them,

2 That the sons of God saw the daughters of men that they *were* fair; and they took them wives of all which they chose.

3 And the LORD said, My spirit shall not always strive with man, for that he also *is* flesh: yet his days shall be an hundred and twenty years.

4 There were giants in the earth in those days; and also after that, when the sons of God came in unto the daughters of men, and they bare *children* to them, the same *became* mighty men which *were* of old, men of renown.

5 And GOD saw that the wickedness of man *was* great in the earth, and *that* every imagination of the thoughts of his heart *was* only evil continually.

6 And it repented the Lord that he had made man on the earth, and it grieved him at his heart.

7 And the LORD said, I will destroy man whom I have created from the face of the earth; both man, and beast, and the creeping thing, and the fowls of the air; for it repenteth me that I have made them.

8 But Noah found grace in the eyes of the Lord.

9a These *are* the generations of Noah . . .

Book of the Sons of Noah

9b Noah was a just man *and* perfect in his generations, *and* Noah walked with God.

10 And Noah begat three sons, Shem, Ham, and Japheth.

11 The earth also was corrupt before God, and the earth was filled with violence.

12 And God looked upon the earth, and, behold, it was corrupt; for all flesh had corrupted his way upon the earth.

13 And God said unto Noah, The end of all flesh is come before me; for the earth is filled with violence through them; and, behold, I will destroy them with the earth.

14 Make thee an ark of gopherwood; rooms shalt thou make in the ark, and shalt pitch it within and without with pitch.

15 And this *is the fashion* which thou shalt make it *of*: The length of the ark *shall be* three hundred cubits, the breadth of it fifty cubits, and the height of it thirty cubits.

16 A window shalt thou make to the ark, and in a cubit shalt thou finish it above; and the door of the ark shalt thou set in the side thereof; *with* lower, second, and third *stories* shalt thou make it

17 And, behold, I, even I, do bring a flood of waters upon the earth, to destroy

all flesh, wherein *is* the breath of life, from under heaven; *and* every thing that *is* in the earth shall die.

18 But with thee will I establish my covenant; and thou shalt come into the ark, thou, and thy sons, and thy wife, and thy sons' wives with thee.

19 And of every living thing of all flesh, two of every *sort* shalt thou bring into the ark, to keep *them* alive with thee; they shall be male and female.

20 Of fowls after their kind, and of cattle after their kind, of every creeping thing of the earth after his kind, two of every *sort* shall come unto thee, to keep *them* alive.

21 And take thou unto thee of all food that is eaten, and thou shalt gather *it* to thee; and it shall be for food for thee, and for them.

22 Thus did Noah; according to all that God commanded him, so did he.

7:1 And the LORD said unto Noah, Come thou and all thy house into the ark; for thee have I seen righteous before me in this generation.

2 Of every clean beast thou shalt take to thee by sevens, the male and his female: and of beasts that *are* not clean by two, the male and his female.

3 Of fowls also of the air by sevens, the male and the female; to keep seed alive upon the face of all the earth.

4 For yet seven days, and I will cause it to rain upon the earth forty days and forty nights; and every living substance that I have made will I destroy from off the face of the earth.

5 And Noah did according unto all that the LORD commanded him.

6 And Noah *was* six hundred years old when the flood of waters was upon the earth.

7 And Noah went in, and his sons, and his wife, and his sons' wives with him, into the ark, because of the waters of the flood.

8 Of clean beasts, and of beasts that *are* not clean, and of fowls, and of every thing that creepeth upon the earth,

9 There went in two and two unto Noah into the ark, the male and the female, as God had commanded Noah.

10 And it came to pass after seven days, that the waters of the flood were upon the earth.

11 In the six hundredth year of Noah's life, in the second month, the seventeenth day of the month, the same day were all the fountains of the great deep broken up, and the windows of heaven were opened.

12 And the rain was upon the earth forty days and forty nights.

13 In the self same day entered Noah, and Shem, and Ham, and Japheth, the sons of Noah, and Noah's wife, and the three wives of his sons with them, into the ark;

14 They, and every beast after his kind, and all the cattle after their kind, and every creeping thing that creepeth upon the earth after his kind, and every fowl after his kind, every bird of every sort.

15 And they went in unto Noah into the ark, two and two of all flesh, wherein *is* the breath of life.

16 And they that went in, went in male and female of all flesh, as God had commanded him: and the LORD shut him in.

17 And the flood was forty days upon the earth; and the waters increased, and bare up the ark, and it was lift up above the earth.

18 And the waters prevailed, and were increased greatly upon the earth; and the ark went upon the face of the waters.

19 And the waters prevailed exceed-

Appendix B

ingly upon the earth; and all the high hills, that *were* under the whole heaven, were covered.

20 Fifteen cubits upward did the waters prevail; and the mountains were covered.

21 And all flesh died that moved upon the earth, both of fowl, and of cattle, and of beast, and of every creeping thing that creepeth upon the earth, and every man:

22 All in whose nostrils *was* the breath of life, of all that *was* in the dry *land*, died.

23 And every living substance was destroyed which was upon the face of the ground, both man, and cattle, and the creeping things, and the fowl of the heaven; and they were destroyed from the earth: and Noah only remained *alive*, and they that *were* with him in the ark.

24 And the waters prevailed upon the earth an hundred and fifty days.

8:1 And God remembered Noah, and every living thing, and all the cattle that *was* with him in the ark: and God made a wind to pass over the earth, and the waters asswaged;

2 The fountains also of the deep and the windows of heaven were stopped, and the rain from heaven was restrained;

3 And the waters returned from off the earth continually: and after the end of the hundred and fifty days the waters were abated.

4 And the ark rested in the seventh month, on the seventeenth day of the month, upon the mountains of Ararat.

5 And the waters decreased continually until the tenth month: in the tenth *month*, on the first *day* of the month, were the tops of the mountains seen.

6 And it came to pass at the end of forty days, that Noah opened the window of the ark which he had made:

7 And he sent forth a raven, which went forth to and fro, until the waters were dried up from off the earth.

8 Also he sent forth a dove from him, to see if the waters were abated from off the face of the ground;

9 But the dove found no rest for the sole of her foot, and she returned unto him into the ark, for the waters *were* on the face of the whole earth: then he put forth his hand, and took her, and pulled her in unto him into the ark.

10 And he stayed yet other seven days; and again he sent forth the dove out of the ark;

11 And the dove came in to him in the evening; and, lo, in her mouth *was* an olive leaf pluckt off: so Noah knew that the waters were abated from off the earth.

12 And he stayed yet other seven days; and sent forth the dove; which returned not again unto him any more.

13 And it came to pass in the six hundredth and first year, in the first *month*, the first *day* of the month, the waters were dried up from off the earth: and Noah removed the covering of the ark, and looked, and, behold, the face of the ground was dry.

14 And in the second month, on the seven and twentieth day of the month, was the earth dried.

15 And God spake unto Noah, saying,

16 Go forth of the ark, thou, and thy wife, and thy sons, and thy sons' wives with thee.

17 Bring forth with thee every living thing that *is* with thee, of all flesh, *both* of fowl, and of cattle, and of every creeping thing that creepeth upon the earth; that they may breed abundantly in the earth, and be fruitful, and multiply upon the earth.

18 And Noah went forth, and his sons,

and his wife, and his sons' wives with him:

19 Every beast, every creeping thing, and every fowl, *and* whatsoever creepeth upon the earth, after their kinds, went forth out of the ark.

20 And Noah builded an altar unto the Lord; and took of every clean beast, and of every clean fowl, and offered burnt offerings on the altar.

21 And the Lord smelled a sweet savour; and the Lord said in his heart, I will not again curse the ground any more for man's sake; for the imagination of man's heart *is* evil from his youth; neither will I again smite any more every thing living, as I have done.

22 While the earth remaineth, seedtime and harvest, and cold and heat, and summer and winter, and day and night shall not cease.

9:1 And God blessed Noah and his sons, and said unto them, Be fruitful, and multiply, and replenish the earth.

2 And the fear of you and the dread of you shall be upon every beast of the earth, and upon every fowl of the air, upon all that moveth *upon* the earth, and upon all the fishes of the sea; into your hand are they delivered.

3 Every moving thing that liveth shall be meat for you; even as the green herb have I given you all things.

4 But flesh with the life thereof, *which is* the blood thereof, shall ye not eat.

5 And surely your blood of your lives will I require; at the hand of every beast will I require it, and at the hand of man; at the hand of every man's brother will I require the life of man.

6 Whoso sheddeth man's blood, by man shall his blood be shed: for in the image of God made he man.

7 And you, be ye fruitful, and multiply; bring forth abundantly in the earth, and multiply therein.

8 And God spake unto Noah, and to his sons with him, saying,

9 And I, behold, I establish my covenant with you, and with your seed after you;

10 And with every living creature that *is* with you, of the fowl, of the cattle, and of every beast of the earth with you; from all that go out of the ark, to every beast of the earth.

11 And I will establish my covenant with you; neither shall all flesh be cut off any more by the waters of a flood; neither shall there any more be a flood to destroy the earth.

12 And God said, This *is* the token of the covenant which I make between me and you and every living creature that *is* with you, for perpetual generations:

13 I do set my bow in the cloud, and it shall be for a token of a covenant between me and the earth.

14 And it shall come to pass, when I bring a cloud over the earth, that the bow shall be seen in the cloud:

15 And I will remember my covenant, which *is* between me and you and every living creature of all flesh; and the waters shall no more become a flood to destroy all flesh.

16 And the bow shall be in the cloud; and I will look upon it, that I may remember the everlasting covenant between God and every living creature of all flesh that *is* upon the earth.

17 And God said unto Noah, This *is* the token of the covenant, which I have established between me and all flesh that *is* upon the earth.

18 And the sons of Noah, that went

forth of the ark, were Shem, and Ham, and Japheth: and Ham *is* the father of Canaan.

19 These *are* the three sons of Noah: and of them was the whole earth overspread.

20 And Noah began *to be* an husbandman, and he planted a vineyard:

21 And he drank of the wine, and was drunken; and he was uncovered within his tent.

22 And Ham, the father of Canaan, saw the nakedness of his father, and told his two brethren without.

23 And Shem and Japheth took a garment, and laid *it* upon both their shoulders, and went backward, and covered the nakedness of their father, and their faces *were* backward, and they saw not their father's nakedness.

24 And Noah awoke from his wine, and knew what his younger son had done unto him.

25 And he said, Cursed *be* Canaan; a servant of servants shall he be unto his brethren.

26 And he said, Blessed *be* the LORD God of Shem; and Canaan shall be his servant.

27 God shall enlarge Japheth, and he shall dwell in the tents of Shem; and Canaan shall be his servant.

28 And Noah lived after the flood three hundred and fifty years.

29 And all the days of Noah were nine hundred and fifty years: and he died.

10:1a Now these *are* the generations of the sons of Noah, Shem, Ham, and Japheth . . .

Book of Shem

1b . . . and unto them were sons born after the flood.

2 The sons of Japheth; Gomer, and Magog, and Madai, and Javan, and Tubal, and Meshech, and Tiras.

3 And the sons of Gomer; Ashkenaz, and Riphath, and Togarmah.

4 And the sons of Javan; Elishah, and Tarshish, Kittim, and Dodanim.

5 By these were the isles of the Gentiles divided in their lands; every one after his tongue, after their families, in their nations.

6 And the sons of Ham; Cush, and Mizraim, and Phut, and Canaan.

7 And the sons of Cush; Seba, and Havilah, and Sabtah, and Raamah, and Sabtecha: and the sons of Raamah; Sheba, and Dedan.

8 And Cush begat Nimrod: he began to be a mighty one in the earth.

9 He was a mighty hunter before the LORD: wherefore it is said. Even as Nimrod the mighty hunter before the Lord.

10 And the beginning of his kingdom was Babel, and Erech, and Accad, and Calneh, in the land of Shinar.

11 Out of that land went forth Asshur, and builded Nineveh, and the city Rehoboth, and Calah,

12 And Resen between Nineveh and Calah: the same *is* a great city.

13 And Mizraim begat Ludim, and Anamim, and Lehabim, and Naphtuhim,

14 And Pathrusim, and Casluhim, (out of whom came Philistim,) and Caphtorim.

15 And Canaan begat Sidon his firstborn, and Heth,

16 And the Jebusite, and the Amorite, and the Girgasite,

17 And the Hivite, and the Arkite, and

the Sinite,

18 And the Arvadite, and the Zemarite, and the Hamathite: and afterward were the families of the Canaanites spread abroad.

19 And the border of the Canaanites was from Sidon, as thou comest to Gerar, unto Gaza; as thou goest, unto Sodom, and Gomorrah, and Admah, and Zeboim, even unto Lasha.

20 These *are* the sons of Ham, after their families, after their tongues, in their countries, *and* in their nations.

21 Unto Shem also, the father of all the children of Eber, the brother of Japheth the elder, even to him were *children* born.

22 The children of Shem; Elam, and Asshur, and Arphaxad, and Lud, and Aram.

23 And the children of Aram; Uz, and Hul, and Gether, and Mash.

24 And Arphaxad begat Salah; and Salah begat Eber.

25 And unto Eber were born two sons: the name of one *was* Peleg; for in his days was the earth divided; and his brother's name *was* Joktan.

26 And Joktan begat Almodad, and Sheleph, and Hazarmaveth, and Jerah,

27 And Hadoram, and Uzal, and Diklah,

28 And Obal, and Abimael, and Sheba,

29 And Ophir, and Havilah, and Jobab: all these *were* the sons of Joktan.

30 And their dwelling was from Mesha, as thou goest unto Sephar a mount of the east.

31 These *are* the sons of Shem, after their families, after their tongues, in their lands, after their nations.

32 These *are* the families of the sons of Noah, after their generations, in their nations: and by these were the nations divided in the earth after the flood.

11:1 And the whole earth was of one language, and of one speech.

2 And it came to pass, as they journeyed from the east, that they found a plain in the land of Shinar; and they dwelt there.

3 And they said one to another, Go to, let us make brick, and burn them throughly. And they had brick for stone, and slime had they for morter.

4 And they said, Go to, let us build us a city and a tower, whose top *may reach* unto heaven; and let us make us a name, lest we be scattered abroad upon the face of the whole earth.

5 And the LORD came down to see the city and the tower, which the children of men builded.

6 And the LORD said, Behold, the people *is* one, and they have all one language; and this they begin to do: and now nothing will be restrained from them, which they have imagined to do.

7 Go to, let us go down, and there confound their language, that they may not understand one another's speech.

8 So the LORD scattered them abroad from thence upon the face of all the earth: and they left off to build the city.

9 Therefore is the name of it called Babel; because the Lord did there confound the language of all the earth: and from thence did the Lord scatter them abroad upon the face of all the earth.

10a These *are* the generations of Shem . . .

Appendix B

Book of Terah

10b Shem *was* an hundred years old, and begat Arphaxad two years after the flood:

11 And Shem lived after he begat Arphaxad five hundred years, and begat sons and daughters.

12 And Arphaxad lived five and thirty years, and begat Salah:

13 And Arphaxad lived after he begat Salah four hundred and three years, and begat sons and daughters.

14 And Salah lived thirty years, and begat Eber:

15 And Salah lived after he begat Eber four hundred and three years, and begat sons and daughters.

16 And Eber lived four and thirty years, and begat Peleg:

17 And Eber lived after he begat Peleg four hundred and thirty years, and begat sons and daughters.

18 And Peleg lived thirty years, and begat Reu:

19 And Peleg lived after he begat Reu two hundred and nine years, and begat sons and daughters.

20 And Reu lived two and thirty years, and begat Serug:

21 And Reu lived after he begat Serug two hundred and seven years, and begat sons and daughters.

22 And Serug lived thirty years, and begat Nahor:

23 And Serug lived after he begat Nahor two hundred years, and begat sons and daughters.

24 And Nahor lived nine and twenty years, and begat Terah:

25 And Nahor lived after he begat Terah an hundred and nineteen years, and begat sons and daughters.

26 And Terah lived seventy years, and begat Abram, Nahor, and Haran.

27 Now these *are* the generations of Terah . . .

Appendix C
Study Projects

The following ideas, or adaptations of them, can be used by families, study groups and individuals for learning more about the early world.

1. In Appendix B find the books of God, Adam, Noah, Noah's sons, Shem, and Terah. Read these one at a time, together with your family if possible. Read, also, Appendix A about the meaning of the Hebrew word *toledoth*, which is translated *generations*. Sometimes use the words *beginnings* or *origins* for the word *generations* as you read the closing sentence of each book and see what new thoughts that gives you.

Compare the books of God and of Adam. Which tells most about the first five days of creation? Which tells most about Adam and Eve? The garden of Eden? The descendents of Adam?

Compare the books of Noah and of his sons. What does Noah tell about himself? What do the sons tell about him?

Talk about other matters that your family or study group members notice during these readings.

2. Make a graph of the patriarchs' life spans. First, obtain some graph paper and decide how many years each square will stand for. With tiny squares, 100 years per square works well. Place the names of the patriarchs from Adam to Noah down the left side of

the page. Refer to the text in Genesis 5, and draw a horizontal line after each patriarch to show his life span. Start each line at the year of the man's birth. For instance, Adam's line begins in year 1 and Seth's line begins at Adam's 130th year.

Refer to Genesis 11 if you wish to continue the graph through Abram. It takes more calculation for Shem and Abram than for the others. Consider verse 11:10 together with verse 5:32, and you find that Shem was not the firstborn. (Japheth was, we read in verse 10:21.) From these verses, we see that Shem was born when Noah was 502 years old. To figure Abram's birth, use Genesis 11:32 and 12:4 along with Acts 7:4. Calculate 75 years backward from Terah's death to find Abram's birthdate.

Discuss with your family or friends what the finished chart shows you. Notice the overlapping of life spans. How many direct ancestors could Noah have met? How many generations could Shem have preached to? When do the lifespans became shorter.

3. If you are an older student who already knows the Bible well, you may like analyzing mythology. When you read Greek or other ancient mythical stories, see if you can find ideas in them which come from the original true stories of Genesis or the original pagan stories of Babel. For instance, the story of Pandora tells about the woman Zeus made—the first woman. Her curiosity led her to disobey the gods and open a box which they had forbidden her to open. This let loose upon the world many evils and only one good—Hope. Could this be a distorted version of the original story of Eve? Achilles was vulnerable only in his heel and met his death by an arrow to that spot. That idea could have come from early men who knew the promise in Genesis 3:15.

Hercules was said to be a son of Zeus. He helped Zeus to defeat the Giants and the Titans. The Greek word *Titan* came from the earlier Chaldean word *Teitan*, which meant Satan. The Greek Titans, then, can be seen as the angels of Satan, and much of Greek mythology tells of wars and other doings of these super human beings. The Greek poet, Hesiod, wrote that the Titans eventually were "Bound in bitter chains beneath the wide-wayed earth." (See Jude 6.)

Besides the theme of Satan and his revolt, practically all mythologies have creation themes, trinity themes and others which Bible students can recognize, even though they are much distorted. A family study of these can range from discussing one story, such as Pandora, to a broader literature study of Greek, Roman, Norse or other mythologies. It is recommended that the students first be familiar with the Bible stories, particularly those of creation, the fall, and the Flood.

4. Read from the books listed in this bibliography, or other books, to learn more about any questions you may have. Examples: 1) Does the word *day* in Genesis 1 have a figurative meaning, or does it mean a literal day bounded by "the evening and the morning?" Some arguments are in *The Genesis Record* by Henry Morris, pages 53-54. 2) Did ancient peoples have the ability to pour "stone?" See *The Pyramids* by Joseph Davidovitz and Margie Morris.

Write down your questions when they come to you, and use your study time to search for answers.

5. Here is a lifetime project for serious student historians. Learn more about the Sumerians. Learn to read their writings and help to translate some of the thousands of tablets stored at the University of Pennsylvania and elsewhere. You may be the person who closes the "history gap"—the period of time just after the Tower of Babel, about which we now have no clear historical records.

Appendix D
Annotated Bibliography

To keep this list within bounds only some old books and others particularly used for the present work in one way or another are included. Numerous other books of Bible commentary, archaeology, astronomy, ancient civilizations and mythology were also used and could be helpful to readers wishing to pursue any of these topics further. Many such can be found in public libraries, but the best books on the most ancient of civilizations and languages are to be found in seminary or university libraries. One public librarian apologetically said, "We have materials through college level, but not on the postgraduate level." Evidently the Greeks are for undergraduate study, but the Sumerians are for later study!

Allen, Richard Hinckley, *Star Names: Their Lore and Meaning.* New York, Dover, 1963. A corrected republication of a work of 1899 by G. E. Stechert under the title of *Star-Names and Their Meanings.* Detailed compendium of star and constellation names as far back in history as the Chaldeans. Arabic and Greek index, and general English index.

Angus, Samuel, *The Mystery-Religions and Christianity.* New York, Charles Scribner's Sons, 1925. A good survey of the beliefs and practices of ancient mystery religions, although the discussion treats them as steps toward the true religion rather than as outgrowths of original paganism.

Bullinger, E. W., *The Witness of the Stars*. Grand Rapids, Kregal, 1967. A reprint of an 1893 edition published in London. Uses the most ancient information available as collected by Frances Rolleston, and interprets the meaning of star and constellation names to try to reach true beginnings for the ancient astronomical systems.

Cooper, Bill, *After the Flood*. Chichester, England, New Wine Press, 1995. Without access to the Book of Genesis, ancient historians from five nations in pre-Christian Europe independently traced their ancestry back to Noah. Cooper has gathered and summarized many of these records for us. Also numerous historical reports of dragons from ancient to quite recent times. A chapter on Beowulf shows it to contain historic characters and real, dinosaur-like monsters with zoological names, rather than the mythical names most translators use.

Davidovits, Joseph and Morris, Margie, *The Pyramids: An Enigma Solved*. New York, Hippocrene Books, 1988. Proposes, with much scientific evidence, that many of the large early pyramids, as well as stone vessels, were of cast stone rather than cut or carved stone. Thus, it would not take the lifetime of a craftsman to carve one bowl which only the very wealthy could afford, as former guesses indicated. And the use of stoneware, then, fits into a common sense view of early Mesopotamian civilizations.

Hislop, Alexander, *The Two Babylons*. Neptune, New Jersey, Loizeaux Brothers, 1959 (published in England by A & C Black, Ltd.). First published in 1916. A study of ancient paganism, from its roots at Babel and the time of Nimrod through the papal system, and on to the events prophesied in the book of Revelation. Takes the view that Rome is mystical Babylon—a second Babylon.

James, Peter, *Centuries of Darkness*. Rutgers University Press, 1993. Proposes that our dating of Greece and surrounding civilizations before about 800 BC is in error because of our dependence upon faulty Egyptian dates. By putting this history together using 20th century archeology knowledge and ignoring Egyptian dating, James would shorten ancient history by several centuries. This solves innumerable problems that archeologists have had, and it brings history into alignment with the Bible. "By redating the beginning of the Iron Age in Palestine from the early 12th century BC to the late 10th, a completely new interpretation of the archaeology of Israel can be offered: one which is in perfect harmony with the biblical record. The search for the riches of Solomon's reign can be brought to an end—they have already been found, but simply not recognized, in the material remains of the Late Bronze Age." This alignment with the Bible was an unsought conclusion, not a starting point in the investigation. The book is heavy with technical archeological material, but serious students of these times will find it invaluable.

King, L. W., *The Seven Tablets of Creation*. London: Luzac and Co., 1902. Later tablets than are discussed in Kramer's book on Sumerian mythology, but they show again how closely a war in heaven was associated with creation in the minds of the ancients.

Kramer, Samuel Noah, *Sumerian Mythology*. Philadelphia: University of Pennsylvania Press, 1972. One of the greatest of Assyriologists presents text and essays about some of the earliest Sumerian literary compositions. These may bring us closer to original pagan beliefs than the more garbled mythology of the Greeks and Romans. The primeval sea is "the mother who gave birth to all the gods." Themes of creation and dragon-slaying are closely connected, and are universal, as are themes of a flood; and one thesis of this book is that these stories did not originate with Moses and the Hebrews, or even with the Babylonians, but with the Sumerians. (A view of Adam and Noah as real people with a literary tradition predating all of those is not considered.)

Other books by Kramer are also useful for studying the Sumerians.

Lemmer, Uwe, "Neuere Betrachtrungen zum Stern von Bethlehem" (New Observations on the Star of Bethlehem). *Sterne und Weltraum*, vol. 19, Dec. 1980, p. 405-406. These "new" observations do not refer to astronomical information but to historical information concerning Herod's death possibly occurring in the year 0 instead of about three years earlier as commonly assumed. Thus Jesus could have been born in —1, and events in the sky at that time hold exciting possibilities for study.

Maunder, E.Walter, *The Astronomy of the Bible*. London: T. Sealey Clark, 1908. A famous astronomer with competence also in ancient history and languages treats with reverence all Scripture passages relating to astronomy. He occasionally bows to the higher criticism of his day, and he wrote without benefit of recent researches in the field of Bible and science; nevertheless this is one of the most valuable resources on this topic.

Michanowsky, George, *The Once and Future Star*. New York, Hawthorne Books, 1977. Tells of the supernova Vela X, which must have been the most spectacular stellar event of ancient times, appearing for several months almost as large as our sun or moon. With new scientific knowledge about this super nova, cuneiformists may have to retranslate some formerly puzzling texts to find what the ancients might have said about it.

Morris, Henry, *The Genesis Record*. Grand Rapids, Baker Book House, 1976. Verse-by-verse commentary of Genesis by the founder of the modern Bible science movement. Essential for any student of the early world.

Morris, Henry, *The Long War Against God*. Grand Rapids, Baker Book House, 1989. Though not used in preparation of the present work because it appeared after this was finished, we are making a last minute addition to the bibliography of this important book because in scholarly fashion it traces paganism backward to its origin at Babel, a theme which this present book attempts to show in narrative style. For serious study of the history of pagan thought (with its evolutionism), *The Long War* will be the definitive work for years to come.

Mosely, John, *The Christmas Star.* Los Angeles, Griffith Observatory, 1987. Explains several theories about what it was the wise men saw in the sky, including the one defended in the Lemmer article, above. (Griffith Observatory, 2800 Observatory Road, Los Angeles CA 90027. Mail order cost: $5)

Pember, George Hawkins, *Earth's Earliest Ages*. Grand Rapids, Kregal, 1975. First published in England in 1876, then republished and re-edited several times before reaching this edition. Makes a good supplement to the Hislop book, as it describes Spiritualism, Theosophy and Buddhism and shows how these are similar to the satanic demonism of Noah's time. Has the "gap" view that there are long ages between Genesis 1:1 and 2, which was a popular view in Pember's time.

Rich, Claudius, "Was Babylon Here?" in *Hands on the Past* by C.W. Ceram (New York: Alfred A. Knopf). This selection is reprinted from an 1818 book by Rich, first published in London. It analyzes available ancient writings on the Tower of Belus in the light of his own on-site observations and comes to a conclusion concerning its location different from what other writers had said.

Seiss, Joseph, *The Gospel in the Stars*. Philadelphia: Castle Press, 1884. An American Bible scholar, preceding Bullinger, undertook a similar work of reinterpreting ancient astronomical information. He, also, depended largely on the collection work of Frances Rolleston—*Mazzaroth*; or, *The Constellations*.

Vanderburgh, Frederick Augustus, *Sumerian Hymns*. New York: The Columbia University Press, 1908. A translation and commentary of hymns to Bel and other gods of the old Babylonians. Gives insight into the beliefs and thinking of these early pagans.

Velikovsky, Immanuel, *Worlds in Collision*. New York, Doubleday, 1950. A history of earthly and astral catastrophes, which the author places in the times of Moses and Joshua and in the seventh and eighth centuries B.C.

Woolley, C. Leonard, *Ur of the Chaldees*. New York: Charles Scribner's Sons, 1930. A standard, older work on Ur by a leading excavator of the site.

Woolley, C. Leonard, *The Sumerians*. New York, London: W. W. Norton & Co., 1965. A reprint of an older Oxford University book. Summarizes what was known or thought about the Sumerians during the first half of the twentieth century. Includes the ancient "king lists" which are referred to in many books but are not often printed in them.